Changing Commands

The Betrayal of America's Military

John F. McManus

The John Birch Society
Appleton, Wisconsin

First Printing.....................March 1995

Published by
The John Birch Society
Post Office Box 8040
Appleton, Wisconsin 54913
(414) 749–3780

Printed in the United States of America
Library of Congress Catalog Card Number: 95–075910
ISBN: 1–881919–03–X

Dedication

To all who have proudly and honorably worn the uniform of this nation, especially those who have put their lives on the line in combat, and most especially to any who paid the supreme sacrifice so that the rest of us could remain free, we dedicate this book.

There is no finer tribute to these wonderful Americans than the one given by General of the Army Douglas MacArthur during his farewell speech at West Point on May 12, 1962.

With enduring gratitude to all who have served, and with special thanks to that military genius whose sense of "duty, honor, country" will forever inspire all who call themselves American, we offer General MacArthur's description of the American Man at Arms:

> My estimate of him was formed on the battlefield many years ago, and has never changed. I regarded him then as I regard him now — as one of the world's noblest figures, not only as one of the finest military characters, but also as one of the most stainless. His name and fame are the Birthright of every American citizen. In his youth and strength, his love and loyalty, he gave all that mortality can give. He needs no eulogy from me or from any other man. He has written his own history and written it in red on his enemy's breast. But when I think of his patience under adversity, of his courage under fire, and of his modesty in victory, I am filled with an emotion of admiration I cannot put into words. He belongs to history as furnishing one of the greatest examples of successful patriotism; he belongs to posterity as the instructor of future generations in the principles of liberty and freedom; he belongs to the present, to us, by his virtue and by his achievements. In twenty campaigns, on a hundred battlefields, around a thousand campfires, I have witnessed that enduring fortitude, that patriotic self-abnegation, and that invincible determination which have carved his status in the hearts of his people. From one end of the world to the other he has drained the deep chalice of courage.

Contents

Contents

Introduction

I would swear to the following code: "I am a United Nations fighting person. I serve in the forces which maintain world peace and every nation's way of life. I am prepared to give my life in their defense."

— Combat Arms Survey administered to U.S. Marine Corps personnel based at Twentynine Palms, California
May 10, 1994

The first reaction of most Americans to the warning that our nation's armed forces are being taken from U.S. control and placed under the United Nations might well be one of incredulity. But if no such plan exists, why were hundreds of Marine Corps personnel forced to participate in the May 10, 1994 survey in which they were asked to register their opinion about the above statement? Why did that survey ask for their attitudes about dozens of other new and revolutionary uses of their efforts, many of which involve making them subject to the United Nations? What's going on here?

The survey asked the Marines to check off whether they strongly disagree, disagree, agree, strongly agree, or have no opinion. About what? To begin with, about the use of U.S. "combat troops" for such missions in this nation as drug enforcement, disaster relief, security at public events, substitute teaching, serving as prison guards, as national emergency police, etc.

It then asked for their opinion about the propriety of assigning U.S. combat troops to carry out these same types of missions in other countries a) "under U.S. command," and b) "under command of non-U.S. officers appointed by the United Nations."

The next section of this survey posed the following subversive attitudes and asked the young Marines for their opinion about each:

• "I feel the President of the United States has the authority to pass his responsibilities as Commander-in-Chief to the U.N. Secretary General."

- "I feel there is no conflict between my oath of office and serving as a U.N. soldier."
- "I feel my unit's combat effectiveness would not be affected by performing humanitarian missions for the United Nations."
- "I feel a designated unit of U.S. combat soldiers should be permanently assigned to the command and control of the United Nations."
- "I would be willing to volunteer for assignment to a U.S. combat unit under a U.N. commander."
- "I would like U.N. member countries, including the U.S., to give the U.N. all the soldiers necessary to maintain world peace."
- "I would swear to the following code: 'I am a United Nations fighting person. I serve in the forces which maintain world peace and every nation's way of life. I am prepared to give my life in their defense.'"

What a superb way to undermine the patriotism of young men serving their country! What an excellent technique to prepare them for transfer to the United Nations!

But not only was this survey loaded with scenarios promoting the subjugation of our nation's armed forces to the United Nations, it took deadly aim at a key element of the American system. The last item the Marines were asked to comment about was this outrageous scenario:

> The U.S. government declares a ban on the possession, sale, transportation, and transfer of all non-sporting firearms. A thirty (30) day amnesty period is permitted for these firearms to be turned over to the local authorities. At the end of this period, a number of citizen groups refuse to turn over their firearms. Consider the following statement: I would fire upon U.S. citizens who refuse or resist confiscation of firearms banned by the U.S. government.

Fire on citizens who refuse to give up their firearms? This scenario conveys the notion that the U.S. government has the authority to ban the private ownership of firearms.

What about the God-given right, guaranteed by the Second Amendment, of Americans to own firearms — the same Second Amendment which is part of the Constitution each member of the armed forces swears to uphold? Doesn't the Declaration of Independence proclaim the "self-evident" truth that men are "endowed by their Creator with certain unalienable Rights," one of which is self-defense — the right to keep and bear arms?

Whose interests are served by suggesting that the United Nations is more important than the American system, or that the President can turn over his responsibilities as Commander in Chief to the UN Secretary-General? This survey is chock full of poison.

In years gone by, senior officers at any U.S. military base would have refused permission to anyone seeking to have the men in their command participate in such a survey. They would have demanded that higher authorities discipline any military personnel attempting such a stunt. But the officers at the Twentynine Palms Marine base cooperated fully with the Navy lieutenant commander who authored it, and they cooperated further by ordering the Marines brought before him to take part in it.

Only three months earlier, the senior Marine Corps officers at the Twentynine Palms installation had welcomed to the post a 40-member delegation from the privately run Council on Foreign Relations (CFR). According to the March 1994 issue of the post newspaper, base commander Brigadier General Russell H. Sutton called the visit "an excellent opportunity to display the training conducted aboard the Combat Center as well as the capabilities of the operating forces stationed here." The article said that CFR personnel were transported around the facility "by CH-53 helicopters to observe various aspects of training."

Why is the Marine Corps giving a red carpet tour to the premier U.S. organization promoting world government under the United Nations? (See Appendix A for an explanation of the history and purposes of the Council on Foreign Relations.) Doesn't this action suggest that a drastic alteration of the mission of the armed services is in the works? The very presence of this CFR contingent on a military post suggests a decided shift towards its goals and away from the traditional role of the armed forces.

Why was there no outrage from the Marine officers in charge — about the survey or about the CFR visit? Part of the answer has to be that the commandant of the Marine Corps, General Carl E. Mundy Jr., holds membership in the CFR. So do several of his colleagues among the Joint Chiefs of Staff. (chapter 11 contains an analysis of CFR domination at the top echelons of each branch of the U.S. armed services.) Their membership in the CFR suggests that these men are at least being groomed to accept world government and the transfer of the forces under their command to UN control. If any senior military official should decide to oppose these plans, he knows he would be objecting to what many of his superiors favor. He would, in effect, be asking for the end to personal advancement, probably even his career.

In days gone by, all of the men who led our nation's armed services placed the importance of their oath above all other pledges. They swore to "support and defend the Constitution of the United States against all enemies foreign and domestic." But as we show in the pages that follow, our nation can no longer expect such an attitude, either from many of our military commanders or from many of our political officials.

Warnings About Conspiracy

In recent years, many well-documented books have warned about political treachery, the destruction of the dollar, the subversiveness of the government's education program, the tyranny of rapidly expanding bureaucratic rule, and many other critically important matters affecting the well-being of the American people and the health of this nation. (See the recommended reading list appearing in the final pages of this book.)

The authors of these valuable works concluded that our nation's ills have not resulted from bad luck or incompetence on the part of well-meaning leaders. They point, instead, to conspiracy, to deliberate destructiveness, and to downright evil in our midst.

What about our nation's military? Could the same forces be at work to subvert its mission and its very existence? The answer is an emphatic yes.

Steps being taken to subvert the U.S. military and to transfer it to UN control stretch back over many years. They include:

• Using war both to build the power of government and to make the American people more dependent on it.

• Converting the people's revulsion for war into support for world government.

• Disarming this nation and turning its remaining armed forces over to United Nations control.

• Recruiting military professionals into world-government-promoting organizations and having these individuals lead the armed services.

• Demoralizing good men and driving many out of the armed services by opening up the military to homosexuals and by placing women in combat roles.

• Transferring exclusive power to declare war from Congress to the Executive Branch, and distorting the intended meaning of the President's designation as Commander in Chief.

• Entangling America in alliances, pacts, and treaties that rob it of the ability to act in its own interests.

• Expending American lives and treasure in conflicts where there is no national interest or security threat.

• Converting our military into the UN's globocop.

• Compelling units of our armed services to enforce government edicts aimed at destroying the freedom of the American people.

• Creating an all-powerful and unchallengeable world government at the United Nations — led by the same conspirators who seek to destroy America.

Everything we have just listed either has been or is being accomplished. America is suffering from a massive betrayal, a destructiveness orchestrated by powerfully organized plotters — a sinister campaign that becomes obvious to anyone who takes the time to look at the evidence.

Who benefits from the many changes in the traditional uses of our nation's military? Certainly not the nation itself. Nor do those who fly the planes, man the ships, and carry the rifles. The beneficiaries are those determined to bring this nation into their "new world order," the participants in a conspiratorial drive working to establish an "order" where nations no longer exist and where individual freedom is only a memory.

If the plans of this conspiracy aren't exposed and blocked, our nation will soon cease to exist. The United States of America will become one of many administrative units taking orders from a world government. Americans who resist will face heavily armed blue-helmeted UN troops arriving on our shores to enforce the will of their master. Such a UN mission may even include some Americans, but they will be the kind whose loyalty to this nation and its people can be bought.

The final curtain has not come down on America. Our nation and its glorious traditions and unmatched freedoms can still be preserved. All that has been lost can be regained. All that is threatened can be protected. But time is running out. In the 21st century, no nation will exist in freedom for very long without full control of its own armed forces. Yet America's leaders are rapidly giving up control to the United Nations.

Several centuries before Christ, a renowned prophet lamented that his people had been "led away captive because they had not knowledge." (Isaiah 5:13.) Americans need a solid dose of knowledge to avoid being made captive. They have to know who their enemy is, the danger of allowing a world government to be built around them, why their nation is worth fighting for, and what can be done to save it.

The pages that follow were written to fill this need. Now that you have this book, you can never say you weren't told.

CHAPTER 1

Changing the Role of America's Armed Forces

The Clinton Administration appears dedicated to sending the U.S. military into dangerous seas of multinational peace-keeping in an effort to elevate the status of the United Nations into a guardian arbiter of the new world order ... [with] a new world army whose singular purpose is to enforce the whims of the arcane United Nations Security Council.

— Senator Trent Lott (R-MS), October 5, 1993

Any person who joins the armed forces of this nation swears an oath to the U.S. Constitution. Traditionally, virtually all who put on the uniform of this nation's military have served with singular honor, in keeping with the understanding that their total mission was to protect the lives and property of the people of this nation. Maintaining the sovereignty of the United States of America has always been a fundamental part of that mission.

Except for the War Between the States, for more than two centuries, our military forces have operated from the belief that America's only enemies are outside our borders. It is difficult for a military professional, even more so than the average civilian, to conclude that an enemy lurks within, and especially within the military itself. Yet, this is the reality in America today.

Our fighting men went off to the Pacific after Japan attacked Pearl Harbor on December 7, 1941. More men went off to Europe when Germany declared war on our nation a few days later. Why? Because our nation and its people — the families of these men included — were threatened by a foreign enemy. There was a need to fight to insure that our nation would remain free and independent.

Lately, however, the military's role has been significantly altered to include a new category of national responsibility, that of protecting the undefined "vital interests of the United States." That phrase is broad enough to cover just about anything a President might want. And recent Presidents have employed this very phrase to justify dispatching troops to the far corners of the earth and to use them to enforce resolutions of the United Nations. This is dangerously wrong.

America's Chief Executives have in recent years told the people that our "vital interests" call for injecting U.S. military might — under UN auspices — into an attempted takeover of one Arab nation by another, a civil war in faraway Somalia, a centuries-old territorial struggle in the former Yugoslavia, and a totally domestic fight for leadership in Haiti. Practically everything on earth has become a U.S. concern — but always under UN jurisdiction.

No matter what the President says, however, such missions are not constitutionally authorized. Any American who feels compelled to defend one side or another in any of these conflicts is free to volunteer his or her own services, but not free to force others to participate or to pay with tax dollars for such ventures.

The U.S. military was not created to be a mercenary force for sale to the highest bidder. It is not supposed to act as a worldwide service club performing good deeds around the globe. And no President has the legitimate authority to make our armed forces available to a world government. The U.S. military is a taxpayer-supported force whose role is limited by the Constitution of the United States to the defense of the lives and property of our people and the independence of our nation.

Over the years, Congress has allowed some fundamental and frightening changes regarding the military. Resistance to this steady transformation — both in and out of the services — has been slight, or at least not reported. So the changes have been accepted and various steps along this suicidal route have become U.S. policy. Unless such dangerous policies are reversed, they will result in the conversion of our nation's armed forces into a full-fledged UN military force. And the American people will see an end to their freedom.

Softening up the Troops

After the text of the May 10th survey at the Twentynine Palms Marine Corps base had been confirmed by one of the Marines who was forced to participate, information about it appeared in *The New American* magazine.[1] Military officials who were questioned about it quickly insisted that the project was the sole work of its creator, Navy Lieutenant Commander Guy Cunningham, a master's degree student at the Naval Postgraduate School (NPS) in Monterey, California. They said his project had no official status, and that they were simply helping him so he could write his thesis.

But an official press release issued by NPS stated: "The student's idea for the thesis originated from the Department of Defense's Bottom Up Review, which included a section on peace-keeping, disaster relief, humanitarian assistance, and peace enforcement operations, and from Presidential Review Directives 13 and 25, *which directed DOD to create a U.S. military force structure whose command and control would include the United Nations.*" (Emphasis added.)

So, the Department of Defense (DOD) has indeed been directed by presidential decrees to create the kind of force structure the survey discussed. According to the NPS release, DOD has also been given presidential directives to alter the military's "command and control structure" to include a role for the United Nations. All of this, as we demonstrate in chapter 3, is leading our nation to a condition of having no military force except that which serves the UN.

A reporter for the California-based publication *F&H News* interviewed Lieutenant Commander Cunningham, who maintained that the idea for his survey came from "a magazine article dealing with President Clinton's apparent willingness to place U.S. military combat troops under United Nations command."

Cunningham did not name the magazine, but his assessment of Mr. Clinton's "willingness" was deadly accurate.

Cunningham emphatically insisted that he merely intended to discover how Marines felt about being assigned "non-traditional" roles. He had obviously become aware of the revolutionary changes being foisted on our military. Even if his claims about his motivations are completely honest, Marine Corps senior officers should never have allowed him to proceed with such a survey. It couldn't help but undermine morale, patriotism, and the ultimate effectiveness of the troops.

But senior officers did allow the survey. At some higher levels in the Marine Corps, it is now considered acceptable to have Marine Corps personnel think about all kinds of "non-traditional" roles, including assignments in which they would fire on U.S. citizens. In other words, Marines are being programed to accept assignments that no one wearing an American military uniform should ever be forced to accept. They are even being led to transfer their loyalty to the United Nations.

Non-Traditional Roles

As the following list shows, new roles mentioned in the notorious Twentynine Palms survey are already being introduced in all of the services:

• In June 1993, the U.S. Army issued *FM-105 Operations*, a document outlining a new emphasis on "conducting operations other than war." An entire chapter of this new set of guidelines dwells on peacekeeping missions, humanitarian assistance, disaster relief, riot control, and relations with nations in need of democratic assistance. The document's declaration that "the Army will not operate alone" indicates that the other services will participate in the new assignments.

• During the summer of 1993, President Clinton issued Presidential Decision Directive 13 (PDD-13), which called for rapid expansion of "the United Nation's ... peace enforcement operations around the world." Even the pro-UN *New York Times* commented that PDD-13's intention to place American forces under foreign commanders in UN operations amounted to a significant departure from "long-standing tradition."

• On September 23, 1993, Representative William Goodling (R-PA), the appointed congressional delegate to the United Nations, sent a strongly worded letter to President Clinton, hurriedly signed by 32 House colleagues, expressing "serious reservations" about the Clinton plans contained in PDD-13. Goodling and his fellow representatives stated:

> This proposal appears to coincide with the apparent effort on the part of the U.N. to redefine itself and expand its mission to include not simply peacekeeping, also on a more expanded scope, but also peacemaking and the nexus of "nation building."...
>
> By issuing a blank check committing U.S. troops to the U.N. under foreign command, you would in effect be making U.N. initiatives U.S. commitments, and U.N. conflicts U.S. conflicts, while forfeiting the leadership of the troops on the ground.

The planned transfer of control of our own military had begun to become obvious to some members of Congress.

• On October 5, 1993, Senator Trent Lott (R-MS) saw a larger and more sinister motive in the President's directives. He stated: "The Clinton Administration appears dedicated to sending the U.S. military into dangerous seas of multinational peacekeeping in an effort to elevate the status of the United Nations into a guardian arbiter of the new world order ... [with] a new world army whose singular purpose is to enforce the whims of the arcane United Nations Security Council. The Administration's effort to create a new vision for the U.S. military is embodied in ... PDD-13." Senator Lott hit the nail right on the head. His side-by-side use of the phrases "new world order" and "new world army" indicates that he fully grasps the all-encompassing seriousness of the President's plans.

• On May 3, 1994, President Clinton signed Presidential Decision Directive 25 (PDD-25) and immediately classified it "secret." Simultaneously, National Security Adviser Anthony Lake (CFR) released an official "summary" of the document. It states that U.S. military forces can be placed under foreign command in UN operations "on a case by case basis." If the "summary" admits this much, it seems clear that the document itself must contain even worse plans and directives for the misuse of the military. Why else keep it hidden from the public and even from Congress?

• On June 9, 1994, then-House Minority Leader Robert Michel (R-IL) sought to amend the 1995 Defense Authorization Act. His amendment called merely for placing "prudent limits" on the President's power to place U.S. forces under foreign command in UN operations. It should have emphatically forbidden the placement of troops in such a position. Opponents of the Michel measure read a letter signed by Secretary of Defense William J. Perry and Joint Chiefs of Staff Chairman General John Shalikashvili which stated, "In sum, we believe this proposed legislation is ill-advised and potentially harmful to the execution of military operations. We urge that the House of Representatives not approve this legislation."

Thanks in part to this betrayal from the top civilian and military leaders of our armed forces, the measure was defeated in the House by a vote of 237 to 185. Which means that most members of the 1994 Congress, along with the nation's highest military officer, see nothing wrong with having foreign commanders in UN operations issuing orders to American forces.

• A July 18, 1994 press release from Camp Pendleton Marine Corps base reported that a detachment of Marines and Navy personnel from Southern California would undergo "urban training" near Sacramento, California. The July 23rd-August 3rd TRUE (**TR**aining in an **U**rban **E**nvironment) program would prepare a military unit to become "America's quick reaction force to safeguard this country's citizens, property, and interests" overseas. As shown in our next chapter, there are ample reasons to speculate that this "quick reaction force" could eventually be used to "fire upon U.S. citizens who refuse or resist confiscation of firearms banned by the U.S. government," as the Twentynine Palms survey suggested.

• The *Washington Post* reported on August 15, 1994 about a new type of "peace maneuvers" for Army regulars at Fort Polk, Louisiana. Part of the training called for Army units to "disarm the militia" while being observed by British and French officers playing the role of UN observers.[2]

• In November 1994, Secretary of Defense William Perry approved a plan to employ military reservists to carry out the growing number of non-traditional missions assigned to our armed forces. According to a report in the *New York Times*, the plan would have "many of the one million members of the National Guard and Reserves of the various armed services spend their annual training time performing real operations, including peacekeeping missions overseas...."[3] Army Chief of Staff General Gordon R. Sullivan (CFR) said he was "very supportive" of the idea. Missions involving peacekeeping are, of course, UN missions.

• One week after the 1994 Republican election-day sweep, incoming House Armed Services Chairman Floyd Spence (R-SC) revealed that "wholesale categories of combat units are in a reduced state of readiness." Secretary of Defense Perry reluctantly agreed with Spence's charges and added that the U.S. military's participation in overseas UN missions had forced defense officials to divert funds originally earmarked for training of stateside units. But Army Chief of Staff General Sullivan told the *Boston Globe* during a November 28th visit to Harvard University that he wasn't concerned about the readiness of the troops under his command.[4] Two days later, however, President Clinton was forced to address this serious decline as he proposed a $25 billion increase in the Pentagon's budget. General Sullivan seems to care only about the readiness of troops serving the UN's interests. The country might be better served if he retired.

A New Type of Commander in Chief

Americans have ample reason to be proud of our country's military history. Numerous uniformed giants have served the nation well, especially when allowed by the President to do their jobs properly. Also, many Presidents themselves proudly wore the uniform of our nation before ascending to the highest office in the land. But like so many other changes in America, the White House is occupied today by a remarkably different kind of Commander in Chief.

When Bill Clinton became eligible for the draft while attending the University of Arkansas in 1969, he did everything fair or foul to avoid serving. In a December 1969 letter to Colonel Eugene Holmes, the university's ROTC commander at the time, the future President expressed his "loathing for the military."

That letter, along with a 1992 affidavit submitted by Holmes and additional evidence unearthed during the 1992 campaign, show that Mr. Clinton: a) used dishonorable means on several occasions to evade the draft; b) likely committed a felony in the process; and c) repeatedly lied about what he had done. But because he later became a committed CFR member, his disgraceful conduct was swept aside after it had been discovered, and he became the President of our nation.

After he entered the White House, Bill Clinton filled his Administration with individuals having a similar "loathing" for the military. In late January 1993, only days after the new Administration took office, Lieutenant General Barry McCaffrey, an assistant to the chairman of the Joint Chiefs of Staff, offered a pleasant "Good morning" to a young female Clinton aide on the White House grounds. She promptly rebuked him and told him that her personal policy was not to talk to anyone in a military uniform. What an outrage![5]

With Bill Clinton in the White House, morale in the military has sunk to such depths that an active duty senior officer sacrificed his career by publicly offering an attitude about the President shared by most others in the services. During a formal speech before a military audience in Germany four months after the Clinton inauguration, Air Force Major General Harold N. Campbell labeled the President a "pot-smoking ... gay-loving ... draft-dodging ... and womanizing Commander in Chief."[6]

General Campbell was fined, demoted, and forced to retire. But nothing he stated could be denied. Having a man like Bill Clinton in the White House has taken a significant toll on the morale of those who serve.

In May 1994, President Clinton awarded the Congressional Medal of Honor posthumously to two American soldiers killed during the ill-advised military action in Somalia. Mr. Herbert Shugart, the father of an Army sergeant who perished trying to rescue a downed helicopter pilot, refused to shake the President's hand when presented with his dead son's award. He told the President: "You are not fit to be President of the United States. The blame for my son's death rests with the White House and you. You are not fit to command."[7]

Nor is the office of Vice President in better hands. As a student at Harvard, Al Gore wrote to his father, then a senator from Tennessee, to express the view that the national aversion to communism was "paranoia," "a psychological ailment," and "national madness." He characterized the U.S. Army as an example of "fascist, totalitarian regimes." He later served in the Army on the way to a political career.[8]

Now as Vice President, he has become far more approving of the U.S. military as long as it serves the United Nations. When 15 Americans perished on April 14, 1994 as a result of an attack by friendly fire while they were performing a patrol mission over Iraq, Gore extended official "condolences to the families of *those who died in the service of the United Nations*." (Emphasis added.)

In his report about this incredible statement, columnist Robert Novak stressed that these remarks by the Vice President were "prepared, not impromptu." He noted that this was only one indication that Clinton Administration leaders, "distrustful and resentful of this country acting on its own in the past, truly want a new world order."[9]

The new world order is precisely where our nation is being taken — a redesigned world where the United Nations will reign supreme. Wherever they can, the President and his team will assign our military to the United Nations. They are serving a conspiracy the ultimate goal of which is to create a UN-led world government led by a powerful few. The rest of mankind is slated for slavery — or extinction.

But keeping our nation independent and retaining full U.S. control of our own armed forces isn't just a nice idea, but an absolute necessity. Many more committed Americans are needed in the fight to block the sinister plans unfolding right before our eyes.

The first goal of anyone who wants to "take our country back" must be sharing sufficient information with fellow Americans to have them bring about a change in Congress. The nation sorely needs an influx of elected officials who are uncompromising Americans fully committed to their oath to the U.S. Constitution. A majority of truly informed and determined Americans in the House of Representatives alone can put a stop to the betrayal of the military, and of the nation itself.

This book has been written in hopes that many more Americans will be energized to accomplish such a goal. There is no alternative to rescuing our nation from the clutches of the Conspiracy that has, for too long, been advancing steadily toward its malevolent objectives.

Please read on as we supply the details about the plot to sacrifice American sovereignty on the altar of the United Nations.

Chapter 2

World Government or American Independence?

Yet the individual is handicapped by coming face to face with a conspiracy so monstrous he cannot believe it exists. The American mind simply has not come to a realization of the evil which has been introduced into our midst. It rejects even the assumption that human creatures could espouse a philosophy which must ultimately destroy all that is good and decent.

— FBI Director J. Edgar Hoover
The Elks Magazine, August 1956

Most Americans find it impossible to believe that our leaders are working to strip this nation of its military power. In the view of most, it is also unimaginable that our leaders are planning to transfer both weapons and personnel to a United Nations "Peace Force" which would then possess unchallengeable global power.

Many won't even consider that anything resembling treason could ever occur in this nation. But a mountain of evidence demonstrates very strongly that influential and well-entrenched individuals are indeed conspiring to destroy freedom for all but themselves in their hellish quest for dictatorial power.

Conspiracies Do Exist

The August 1956 issue of *The Elks Magazine* contained an article about the advance of communism throughout our nation. Written by FBI Director J. Edgar Hoover, it took dead aim at the widely held nonsense that communism was simply a misguided ideology. Hoover argued that it was far worse, that it was a monstrous conspiracy determined to conquer America from within.

We don't claim that Hoover's view of conspiracy in 1956 completely coincides with our view in the 1990s. But what he said four decades ago correctly summarizes a problem still hindering Americans today. We offer, again, the pertinent portion of Hoover's 1956 statement which appears at the beginning of this chapter:

> Yet the individual is handicapped by coming face to face with a conspiracy so monstrous he cannot believe it exists. The American mind simply has not come to a realization of the evil which has been introduced into our midst. It rejects even the assumption that human creatures could espouse a philosophy which must ultimately destroy all that is good and decent.

Hoover's argument centers on two main points: 1) A monstrous conspiracy threatens our land; and 2) its existence is habitually discounted because the evil it entails is incomprehensible. Both thoughts capably summarize the situation existing in America today.

Beyond these problems, the American people face an important related obstacle. Many current "experts" ridicule any suggestion that policies and deeds eating away at the soul of America could possibly result from conspiratorial design. Seizing every opportunity to glory in the adulation of the very destroyers they should be exposing, these puffed-up and self-declared shapers of the nation's attitudes steer millions away from resisting the conspiracy's efforts. In the process, they (knowingly or unknowingly) assist the plotters to achieve any effective conspiracy's first goal: to convince others that it doesn't exist.

Franklin Delano Roosevelt once proclaimed, "In politics, nothing happens by accident. If it happens, you can bet it was planned that way." This concept challenges the "accidental theory of history" and certainly suggests the notion of conspiracy.

James Forrestal, our nation's first Secretary of Defense, once commented, "If the diplomats who have mishandled our relations with Russia were merely stupid, they would occasionally make a mistake in our favor." He didn't subscribe to the accidental theory of history, either. The thought he conveyed is that consistency is not a characteristic of stupidity, but of deliberate design. Though he, too, did not use the word conspiracy, his statement surely suggested that one existed.

As we show throughout this book, our nation's independence is being compromised from within and world government is being set up to take its place. Comforting claims that these developments are accidental, an accumulation of bad luck, or attributable to bumblers who are trying but failing to do the best for America simply don't square with the facts.

Attacking U.S. Independence

As the following examples clearly indicate, many advocates of world government have been singing their song for a long time. The following quotes are merely a few of the many that could be presented:

• In their 1958 book entitled *World Peace Through World Law*,[1] Grenville Clark and Louis B. Sohn (CFR) called for a socialist world government including a UN Peace Force possessing "a coercive force of overwhelming power." According to these prominent and influential internationalists, anyone who disagrees with their conclusions is insane:

> It has been well said that in our modern age the obdurate adherence to national sovereignty and national armed forces represents a form of insanity which may, however, be cured by a species of shock treatment.

• In 1959, the Council on Foreign Relations issued its *Study No. 7, Basic Aims of U.S. Foreign Policy*. The document called for the United States to "build a new international order" and to "maintain and gradually increase the authority of the United Nations."

• Walt Rostow (CFR) served the Kennedy Administration as its top official in the State Department's Policy Planning Division.

In 1960, just prior to assuming this strategically important post, he authored *The United States in the World Arena,* in which he called for an end to our nation's independence, arguing that it would be "an American interest to see an end to nationhood as it has been historically defined."[2]

• In a 1960 speech that was widely distributed in pamphlet form, Elmo Roper (CFR) of the Atlantic Union Committee stated:

> For it becomes clear that the first step toward world government cannot be completed until we have advanced on the four fronts: the economic, the military, the political and the social ... the Atlantic Pact [NATO] need not be our last effort toward greater unity. It can be converted into one more sound and important step working toward world peace. It can be one of the most positive moves in the direction of One World.

• In 1961, President John Kennedy delivered to the United Nations his comprehensive *U.S. Program for General and Complete Disarmament in a Peaceful World.* Calling for disarmament and the gradual transfer of our nation's armed forces to the UN, the program foresaw the creation of an unchallengeable UN Peace Force. Incredibly, this program became our nation's policy during the height of the Cold War when the former USSR, in keeping with an agreement at the UN's founding, was authorized to choose the Undersecretary for Political and Security Council Affairs, the UN's chief military official. The overall effect of the Kennedy plan would have had our nation defenseless before a UN army under the command of a Soviet communist. (See chapter 10 for a thorough discussion of this still-unfolding program.) Now that the USSR no longer exists, this plan will have our nation just as defenseless before a UN army ultimately commanded by a Russian "ex-communist."

• In 1962, the State Department produced a taxpayer-funded study entitled *A World Effectively Controlled by the United Nations* authored by CFR member Lincoln P. Bloomfield (CFR).[3] It called for "taxing powers" and a military force "consisting of

500,000 men, recruited individually, wearing a UN uniform" for the contemplated UN world authority. Bloomfield, a professor at MIT, explained:

> "World" means that the system is global, with no exceptions to its fiat: universal membership. "Effectively controlled" connotes ... a relative monopoly of physical force at the center of the system, and thus a preponderance of political power in the hands of a supranational organization.... "The United Nations" is not necessarily precisely the organization as it now exists.... Finally, to avoid endless euphemism and evasive verbiage, the contemplated regime will occasionally be referred to unblushingly as a "world government."

• In 1964, Senator J. William Fulbright (D-AR) proposed the same destructive concept in his book, *Old Myths and New Realities*:[4]

> Indeed, the concept of national sovereignty has become in our time a principle of international anarchy ... the sovereign nation can no longer serve as the ultimate unit of personal loyalty and responsibility.

• In 1974, former State Department official and current U.S. Ambassador to Spain Richard N. Gardner (CFR) authored "The Hard Road to World Order" in *Foreign Affairs,* the flagship journal of the Council on Foreign Relations. No one has ever expressed out-and-out treason more succinctly:

> If instant world government, [United Nations] Charter review, and a greatly strengthened International Court do not provide the answers, what hope for progress is there?... In short, the "house of world order" will have to be built from the bottom up rather than from the top down ... an end run around national sovereignty, eroding it piece by piece, will accomplish much more than the old-fashioned frontal assault.

• In 1978, George Bush (CFR) accepted appointment to the board of the Atlantic Council. This organization's agenda has always included doing away with nation-states such as ours and having "the UN system ... perform the bulk of the global functions." Our nation's Declaration of Independence and Constitution were certain targets of this group's formal Policy Statement, issued on May 10, 1976. The statement, endorsed by Mr. Bush by reason of his seat on the board of the Atlantic Council, declares:

> [The world] can no longer be accommodated by political forms and sovereignties developed in the eighteenth and nineteenth centuries.

• World Federalist Association Vice President John Logue wants UN power to reach right down to every human being, not merely to governments. On December 4, 1985, he told the Human Rights and International Organizations Subcommittee of the U.S. House Foreign Affairs Committee:

> It is time to tell the world's people not what they want to hear, but what they ought to hear ... we must reform, restructure, and strengthen the United Nations and give it the power and authority and funds to keep the peace and promote justice. The Security Council veto must go. One-nation, one-vote must go. The United Nations must have taxing power or some other dependable source of revenue. It must have a large peacekeeping force.... In appropriate areas, particularly in the area of peace and security, it must be able to make and enforce law on the individual.

• Strobe Talbott (CFR), Bill Clinton's roommate at Oxford during their Rhodes Scholar days, was named Deputy Secretary of State in 1993. He showed his disdain for national independence when he penned the following for the July 20, 1992 issue of *Time* magazine:

> ... within the next hundred years ... nationhood as we know it will be obsolete; all states will recognize a single, global authority.

Call the goal of these individuals "the new world order," "world government," or whatever else might come to mind. Whatever you choose to call it, realize that America is being undermined from within. The American people — many of whom sense that something is wrong (but can't put a finger on it) — will be the victims.

World Government Versus Americanism

While many in this nation are uneasy, even apprehensive, about the future, there are others who mistakenly parrot the clichés of the destroyers. You have likely heard some of the following subversive cries:

- "National sovereignty isn't as important as peace!"
- "We live in a global village, not in any particular nation!"
- "World disarmament is essential if there is to be peace!"
- "There has to be a world government!"
- "Our objective must be the creation of a new world order!"

Most of those who echo such drivel aren't as guilty of subversion as those who plant it in the minds of sincere and honest individuals. The originators of these views, however, are deadly enemies. They undermine our nation's independence and pave the way for its destruction as a sovereign entity. They want a world government — and many want it led by themselves.

Confused Americans who place any value in the idea of world government evidently have little appreciation of the fruits of the marvelous heritage we enjoy. They have either forgotten or never knew that our Declaration of Independence starts with the thunderous proclamation that "Men ... are endowed by their Creator with certain unalienable Rights." A search for such a fundamentally sound truth in the roots of other nations will produce nothing even close to that.

The Declaration of Independence, the birth certificate of our nation, holds as a "self-evident" truth that rights are given by God, not by government. It proclaims that "to secure these Rights, Governments are instituted...." In these two assertions can be found the philosophical base upon which this nation was built:

- God exists.
- He endows all persons with certain rights.
- People form governments to protect what God gave them.

In the American view, government wasn't created to redistribute wealth, take control of people's lives, and meddle in their affairs. The true purpose of government is solely and completely the protection of rights. After fighting and winning the War for Independence, our Founders crafted a Constitution to establish a government with strictly limited powers.

Today, world government looms on the horizon, its seat the United Nations — a body that does not recognize God and, therefore, doesn't agree that rights come from Him. Instead, the world body would have everyone believe that it is the grantor of rights.

Then, in its syrupy-sounding Covenant on Civil and Political Rights, the UN repeatedly claims power to restrict what it has supposedly granted. Anyone who reads this UN Covenant will find the declaration, "Everyone shall have the right to freedom of expression." But the document proceeds immediately to state that the exercise of that right "may be subject to certain restrictions ... as are provided by law." When the right to speak freely becomes subject to government-created restrictions, free speech doesn't exist.

The Covenant also discusses freedom of the press, freedom of movement, freedom of religion, and freedom of association. But each freedom noted in this UN document is immediately followed by limitations "as prescribed by law." In other words, these freedoms will be canceled whenever the UN decides to cancel them.

The UN doesn't deal in freedoms; it deals in privileges granted by itself. If history is any guide, privileges granted by government can be and will be suspended.

Because the American system, the complete opposite of the UN's plan, holds that God gives rights to men, our Constitution proclaims that "Congress shall make no law" respecting the rights to speak, publish, practice religion, assemble, petition government, keep and bear arms, etc. What a difference!

Still, the cry is heard, "There must be a world government if there is to be peace." But a world government designed to insure peace must be militarily more powerful than any other nation or group of nations. UN officials already claim that it is their role to "enforce" peace. Yet it is also true that a UN in possession of the world's only unchallengeable military force — able to enforce peace throughout the world — would then have sufficient military power to make the world its slave.

Power corrupts, and creating the kind of military power the United Nations is seeking would be monstrous folly.

If world government were ever to become a reality, it would force the redistribution of the world's wealth. Anyone protesting would face restrictions barring speech, publishing, conducting meetings, even moving about. A world police force or, more likely, a world army would see to it that the world government receives no opposition. A reign of bloodshed and tyranny would spread throughout our land, and all lands. In the end, "peace" would descend — a peace marked by the absence of opposition to the UN. In other words, the peace of submission — which is ultimately the peace of the grave.

"Wake-Up Call" Needed

It is easy to insist that what we are describing can't happen. But it is happening, and doubters ought to look around this nation and note the following:

- Huge numbers of Americans have no appreciation of the marvelous heritage given us by our Founders. Teachers not only don't stress the wonders of the American system, but are actually forbidden to teach it because it includes belief in the Almighty.
- Among many in this nation, the UN Charter is accorded more respect than the U.S. Constitution.
- Recent Presidents have bypassed Congress and cited UN resolutions to send our armed forces into UN-directed combat and peacekeeping missions.
- Our nation is entangled in a host of UN-created international pacts and alliances.
- America's wealth, jobs, and industries are moving overseas,

and our leaders continue to propel the nation into economic unions that are certain steps toward political unions and eventual world government.

• Plans to transform our nation's military into a blue-helmeted UN army, once kept in the shadows, are now openly advocated in the highest circles of government.

These are some of the disturbing developments that should amount to a "wake-up call" for Americans. But the mesmerizing effect of a mass media full of sovereignty haters and UN lovers has taken its toll. Clearly, it is time for Americans from all walks of life and all parts of the nation to realize that their concerns about our nation's direction are based on facts, that their uneasiness about the future isn't a form of paranoia, and that their help is needed if the future is to be marked by freedom instead of by slavery.

Our country is undergoing ominous transitions. Yet, her unique core is still sound. Americans who have the will can still reverse the frightening trends — but they first have to become informed about a multitude of threats and the source of the pressing danger.

While a war rages all about us, most Americans know nothing about it because it is not a shooting war. No cannons or rifles fill the air with smoke and noise; no planes and tanks scream and roar. Instead, this is a total war where the enemy's victories are being piled up in the fields of economics, politics, culture, morality, propaganda, education, and so much more. And, like it or not, we are all involved.

America must not be betrayed. Her promise as the beacon of hope in a world full of strife and treachery must endure. She is still "the land of youth and freedom," as Henry van Dyke so capably and lovingly noted in this portion of his inspiring poem:

'Tis fine to see the Old World, and travel up and down
Among the famous palaces and cities of renown,
To admire the crumbly castles and the statues of the kings,
But now I think I've had enough of antiquated things.

So it's home again, and home again, America for me!
My heart is turning home again, and there I long to be,
In the land of youth and freedom beyond the ocean bars,
Where the air is full of sunlight and the flag is full of stars.

It is America's unrivaled system — not the United Nations — that remains mankind's best hope for peace in this world.

Sad to say, as we show in the next chapter, our nation is being taken — step by step and inch by inch — into a gigantic web being spun for the United Nations by homegrown enemies of America.

Chapter 3

The UN's Noose Tightens

Let me give you this final message. If we use the military, we can make the United Nations a really meaningful, effective voice for peace and stability in the future.

— President George Bush, December 1990[1]

The U.S. Constitution names the President as "Commander in Chief" of the U.S. military. But it does not give him the authority to "use the military" to build the power of the United Nations. A few weeks after he made the above statement, Commander in Chief George Bush gave the order to begin a war against Iraq. As shown later in this chapter, he had already stated on numerous occasions that his objective in doing so was the creation of a "new world order."

The President uttered his underlying goal in sending our troops into Iraq to Senators Paul Simon (D-IL) and George Mitchell (D-ME) at the close of an hour-long visit they made to the White House. The two senators had just returned from a trip to the Middle East where they saw half a million Americans preparing for war. They pleaded with Mr. Bush to negotiate further with Saddam Hussein, give economic sanctions more time to work, or do whatever else he could to avoid the bloodshed they had every reason to expect in the weeks ahead.

Please reread the statement at the top of this chapter carefully. It reveals the President's determination to jeopardize the lives and well-being of American service personnel in a war. He wasn't retaliating for aggression against our nation; there wasn't any. He wasn't about to send them into battle to protect American lives and property; none had been attacked and none were threatened. And it wasn't his intention to order American forces into the Iraq-Kuwait confrontation to defend an ally with whom we were treaty-bound; we had no such commitment to defend Kuwait. Our nation's forces should never have been involved in this fight between Arab neighbors.

So there was no just, reasonable, or constitutional provocation impelling George Bush to use our nation's military forces. Moreover, the way he intended to employ the forces of this nation lay beyond the powers of his office. He would "use the military," he said, to make the United Nations look good, and to build its power and prestige — which is precisely what happened.

All of this should have shocked, outraged, frightened, and disgusted the American people. The President of our nation showed he had little regard for the well-being of our uniformed personnel, and no appreciation of the U.S. Constitution. It was as if the document to which he had sworn a solemn oath didn't even exist.

The American people who failed to protest what he did showed their own disregard for the military and their abysmal ignorance of the President's abuse of his high office. (The Constitution's grant of powers to the President and the Congress are thoroughly examined in subsequent chapters.) Where there should have been a national explosion of revulsion over the President's plans and the weak-kneed congressional abandonment of its responsibilities, there was neither. So Mr. Bush succeeded, and he and others who want a UN-directed world government moved a large step closer to their goal.

During his many years in government service, George Bush frequently was called upon to swear an oath to the Constitution. He did so as a congressman from Texas, as a U.S. ambassador to the UN, as our nation's chief of liaison in China, as director of the CIA, as Vice President, and, finally, as President. But for him, the oath has obviously been a mere formality — as it is for so many government officials who have spent their careers eating away at the Constitution and leading America down the road to world government.

Mr. Bush's unconstitutional use of our armed forces should have been blocked by Congress, and impeachment charges should have been brought against him. But he got away with his treachery because Congress, too, is swarming with those who share his high regard for the UN and his low regard for the Constitution.

When the hostilities ended with only a few American casualties, cheers were heard from coast to coast. But the nation's spirited jubilation wasn't really directed at the President, as he found out 20 months later when his re-election effort went down in flames. The people weren't cheering for George Bush; they were applauding the speedy whipping our military gave to Iraq's ragtag army. But they forgot or never knew that Bush's main goal was boosting the UN.

It may have been reassuring to see proof of our nation's military superiority. It was definitely comforting to know that victory over Iraq had been achieved with so few American casualties. But there shouldn't have been *any* deaths and injuries. Those who understood the underlying purpose of this war knew that, beyond the casualties, upset lives, and enormous expenditure of funds, the cost included strengthening the UN's power and trashing the American system. The independence of America and the freedom of our people took a body blow.

The Law Circumvented

Very few Americans realized that Mr. Bush had cavalierly thumbed his nose at Congress and gone to the United Nations for his authorization to start this war. Some wondered why the entire Congress hadn't complained. Didn't the U.S. Constitution grant Congress the sole power to declare war? If a President can assume powers granted solely to Congress, start a war, and do so for extraconstitutional purposes, hasn't he become the equal of a king? Isn't this precisely what our Founders worked so hard to prevent?

In a clear display of the type of arrogance fit for a monarch, George Bush responded to critics of his plans to bypass Congress as he started the war in Iraq by declaring, "I have the constitutional authority, many attorneys having so advised me."[2] The identity of those "attorneys" has never been revealed. Nevertheless, 54 members of Congress brought suit against the President in a vain attempt to force him to obtain congressional authority before starting the Gulf War.

In 1992, while campaigning for re-election, Mr. Bush displayed his arrogance once again when he boasted to the Texas Republican State Convention, "I didn't have to get permission from some old goat in Congress to kick Saddam Hussein out of Kuwait."[3]

This enormous assumption of power went almost totally unnoticed. And Congress' disgraceful abdication of its role drew little attention. Defenders of the Constitution, however, were justifiably outraged while spokesmen for the world-government-promoting Council on Foreign Relations were not only pleased with these remarkable developments but made sure the full meaning of what had happened wasn't missed.

In an unusual departure from its norm, the CFR journal *Foreign Affairs* led off its first issue of 1991 with an unsigned four-page editorial. Headlined "The Road to War," it stated:

> Never before in American history was there a period quite like it. For 48 days the United States moved inexorably toward war, acting on authority granted by an international organization. On November 29, 1990, in an unprecedented step, the United Nations Security Council authorized the use after January 15, 1991 of "all necessary means" to achieve the withdrawal of Iraqi forces from the territory of Kuwait. On January 12 the Congress of the United States authorized President Bush to use American armed forces to implement that resolution. This too was unprecedented.

Who could disagree? The problem is that precedents such as these are always acted on in the future. Mr. Bush's war to build the UN set the stage for further misuse of the U.S. military for the same purpose.

Building the "New World Order"

President Bush's formal ties to the CFR and its Trilateral Commission spin-off stretch back over many years. For at least two decades, their goals have been his goals.[4] What he had accomplished with his "unprecedented" steps for war in the Middle East meshed totally with the long-held plans of the international socialists from the CFR and elsewhere who are working diligently to build a UN-dominated "new world order."

This high-handed use of our nation's forces did bring about what President Bush termed a "reinvigorated United Nations." Mr. Bush then spent the remaining two years of his term doing everything he could to expand the UN's role, to align more U.S. policies with those of the world body, and to seize upon other opportunities to place our armed forces at its disposal. In effect, he took several major steps to convert the U.S. military into the UN's ready-made globocop, and to allow that globocop free rein throughout the world.

In the months leading up to and after the war with Iraq, Mr. Bush often tipped his hand about the true purpose behind Desert Shield/Desert Storm. Over and over, he stressed the importance of building the image of the United Nations as part of a "new world order." Here are a few of the President's statements:

- **September 11, 1990 televised address:** "Out of these troubled times, our fifth objective — a new world order — can emerge.... We are now in sight of a United Nations that performs as envisioned by its founders."
- **January 7, 1991 interview in *U.S. News & World Report*:** "I think that what's at stake here is the new world order. What's at stake here is whether we can have disputes peacefully resolved in the future by a reinvigorated United Nations."
- **January 9, 1991 press conference:** "And that world order is only going to be enhanced if this newly activated peace-keeping function of the United Nations proves to be effective. That is the only way the new world order will be enhanced."
- **August 1991 *National Security Strategy of the United States*, signed by George Bush:** "In the Gulf, we saw the United Nations playing the role dreamed of by its founders.... I hope history will record that the Gulf crisis was the crucible of the new world order."

Two main points in these pronouncements should be emphasized: 1) Mr. Bush wants a "new world order"; and 2) it will be dominated by the United Nations. It is no secret that the UN was designed from its beginning to be a world government. But his repeated reference to a "new world order" intrigued many.

The phrase isn't the clever concoction of some presidential speechwriter; it has been used throughout the 20th century by schemers and plotters to signify a socialistic slave empire run by a powerful few. Though well understood by both informed proponents and opponents of such a loathsome plan, the phrase had never before been aired so openly. By repeatedly and favorably connecting the two ideas (the United Nations and the new world order), Mr. Bush was making plain the internationalist vision of a UN-based world government.

A super-government sitting atop all mankind has also been the cardinal goal of every communist, socialist, and one-world dreamer, each of whom harbors no loyalty for any nation, and most of whom are anxiously looking forward to the opportunity to enslave mankind. It was just such a collection of individuals who wrote the UN Charter and brought the world organization into existence.[5] And it was a President of the United States, George Bush, who used his office to rescue the UN from its declining power and prestige.

Step-by-Step Building of the UN

In August 1990, when troops were first committed to Operation Desert Shield, Bush Administration spokesmen claimed that the President was acting to defend American interests in the Middle East. But when he later upgraded the military mission, making it offensive in nature and changing its name to Desert Storm, he and Secretary of State James Baker III emphatically rejected the assertion that they needed congressional authorization to launch a war against Iraq.

Early in 1991, only days before the first shots were fired in the conflict, a docile Congress voted (250-183 in the House, 52-47 in the Senate) to authorize the President "to use U.S. Armed Forces pursuant to UN Security Council Resolution 678." Congress alone is granted power under the Constitution to declare war, but this wasn't a declaration of war against Iraq — and no such declaration was warranted. Congress abandoned its authority and submissively caved in to the President, who had boldly asserted his intention to proceed whether he got congressional approval or not.

The shifting of authority here is immense. As *Foreign Affairs* noted in its editorial "The Road to War," two enormously important precedents were established: 1) The President went to the UN for authority to use the U.S. military for war; and 2) Congress sanctioned the President's action. The precedent whereby a President sought permission from the UN to send troops to war without a congressional declaration was obviously part of Mr. Bush's plan to see the UN "reinvigorated."

Previous U.S. military action under the UN umbrella, such as in Korea, started with a UN resolution followed by our nation's willingness to send troops. The sequence in the Iraq war was reversed. The U.S. sent troops to bolster an early UN resolution ordering Iraq out of Kuwait and, after President Bush upgraded the mission from defensive to offensive, he went to the UN for its November 29, 1990 resolution calling for the employment of "all necessary means" to force Iraq out. It wasn't the UN that led the charge in this instance; it was Mr. Bush. Why? He told the world himself that he wanted to see the United Nations become "effective" as a step toward the "new world order."

With these precedents established, the President proceeded during the rest of his term in office to take additional steps that would expand the UN's power and authority. And when George Bush left the White House in January 1993, CFR and Trilateral member Bill Clinton reversed nothing and took even more sovereignty-compromising steps. Here are some of the increasingly significant and frightening developments:

- **U.S. Troops Under Foreign Command in NATO.** On May 29, 1991, Bush Administration Defense Secretary Dick Cheney announced that a sweeping reorganization of NATO will place thousands of American soldiers under German, British, and possibly Belgian command. He termed the move "an important milestone in the transformation of the alliance."[6]

• **President Bush Sanctions New Powers for UN.** On September 23, 1991, Mr. Bush delivered his "Pax Universalis" (Universal Peace) speech at the United Nations. In it, he placed our nation on record as favoring UN military action to settle "nationalist passions" within the borders of any nation. He even sanctioned the use of UN power to remove a nation's leader. It is these newly assumed powers that have been used by the UN in subsequent operations. Never mind that Article 2, Section 7 of the UN Charter forbids UN intervention "in matters which are essentially within the domestic jurisdiction of any state."*

• **UN Bars Congressional Investigation.** On February 29, 1992, U.S. Army Colonel Albert C. Zapanta returned to the United States after a six-month tour of duty with a UN peacekeeping force in Western Sahara. One of 30 Americans sent there to monitor an election, Zapanta had complained about being neglected by the UN, threatened by neighboring Moroccans, and forced to live under dangerous circumstances.

A Senate Foreign Affairs African subcommittee sought to hear Zapanta's testimony about his ordeal. But State Department officials barred his appearance because a UN regulation forbids those who serve in UN missions to give information to national legislatures, even their own. The U.S. had already contributed $43.3 million for this mission. The Bush Administration did nothing to challenge this outrageous UN policy that amounted to another step away from national sovereignty.[7]

• **UN Role Greatly Expanded.** In June 1992, the UN released Secretary-General Boutros Boutros-Ghali's *An Agenda For Peace*. In keeping with the UN's overall intention to rule the nations of the world, Boutros-Ghali began by noting, "The time of

---

* James Wadsworth, U.S. Ambassador to the UN in 1960, noted: "It is a foregone conclusion that had this provision been omitted from the Charter, literally dozens of prospective members in 1945 would have balked at ratification — certainly the United States would have been among them." James J. Wadsworth, *The Glass House: The United Nations in Action* (New York: Frederick A. Praeger, 1966).

absolute and exclusive sovereignty ... has passed." He then called for UN military intervention anywhere in the world to address an entirely new listing of domestic matters within the borders of any nation. According to the Ghali plan, the UN would now confront ecological damage, disruption of family life, unchecked population growth, drug usage, poverty, disease, famine, disparity between rich and poor, virtually anything.

Speaking at the UN on September 21, 1992, President Bush stated: "I welcome the Secretary-General's call for a new agenda to strengthen the United Nations' ability to prevent, contain, and resolve conflict across the globe...." Then, on December 3, 1992, the UN's Security Council declared that the military forces under its jurisdiction could also take action to provide "humanitarian" relief.

• **CIA Forecasts Future UN "Peacekeeping" Operations.** In late 1992, the Directorate of Intelligence of the U.S. Central Intelligence Agency (CIA) issued a report entitled "Worldwide Peacekeeping Operations 1993." Its survey of the entire world identified numerous sites for future or continued UN peacekeeping. These sites included: Cyprus, Croatia, El Salvador, Angola, Somalia, Sudan, Eritrea (Ethiopia), South Ossetia (Georgia), Nagorno-Karabakh, Abkhazia, Sinai, Rwanda, Cambodia, Jerusalem, Western Sahara, Mozambique, Lebanon, the Republic of South Africa, Bosnia-Hercegovina, Haiti, Moldava, Tajikistan, the Golan Heights, Kashmir, Kuwait, Sri Lanka, the Solomon Islands, and Liberia. The awful truth is that, acting on already established precedents which should be overturned, a President could send American forces anywhere at any time with eager UN approval. And he could count on meek compliance from the U.S. Congress.

• **Somalia: A New Type of UN Mission.** In December 1992, one month after he had been soundly defeated for re-election, George Bush sent 30,000 U.S. troops to Somalia in what he claimed was a "humanitarian" mission. Again, he cited a UN resolution for authority — one that he actually asked the UN's Security Council to supply. Again, he had no congressional authorization and, again, there was little congressional outcry.

• **Somali Mission Turns Deadly; Troops Placed Under Foreign Commander.** In a matter of weeks, newly inaugurated President Bill Clinton — at the urging of the UN — upgraded the Somali mission from its humanitarian beginning to a military operation with orders to capture a Somali leader and disarm Somalia's civilian population. UN Secretary-General Boutros-Ghali expressed great satisfaction at the willingness of the U.S. military to be the chief player in the UN's new role of reconstructing a nation. The UN had never before undertaken such a mission.

But when 18 Americans died after being ambushed in October 1993, and U.S. television showed the body of an American G.I. being dragged through Somali streets, some of the bloom faded from the UN rose. What did Mr. Clinton do? He pulled out some of our forces, but put 4,000 troops under the command of Turkish General Cevik Bir, the first time in our nation's history that U.S. combat forces were forced to serve in a UN command under anyone but an American.

• **American Troops Assist Communist Leader.** After first issuing denials, Clinton Administration officials were forced to admit early in 1993 that they had indeed sent members of the U.S. Special Forces to the former Soviet state of Georgia. Their purpose: To assist ex-Soviet Foreign Minister Eduard Shevardnadze's hold on to power he seized after deposing Georgian President Zviad Gamsakurdia. The admission came only after American diplomat Fred Woodruff was killed during the disturbance. Using American troops for such a mission is totally unconstitutional.

• **U.S. Troops Enforce UN Resolutions in Haiti.** In September 1994, President Clinton sent tens of thousands of our nation's troops to Haiti to enforce another UN resolution. Eleven months before this deployment, on October 20, 1993, Senator Jesse Helms (R-NC) sought to amend a Defense Appropriations Act to bar any allocation of funds for military action in Haiti unless Congress approved such action after it received written certification from the President that it was necessary to protect and evacuate American citizens. The Helms amendment was defeated 81-19.

Making the ludicrous claim that internal problems in Haiti posed "a threat to international peace," Mr. Clinton relied on President Bush's previous assumption of power to justify what he was doing. During the first week of August 1993, as he was preparing to give the order for a full-scale military invasion of Haiti (an invasion deemed unnecessary at the last minute), President Clinton responded to a unanimous Senate resolution which sought to block his plans. The senators claimed that the UN's authorization wasn't sufficient and that congressional approval was necessary before the nation could start a war. Mr. Clinton promptly told a news conference, "I would welcome the support of Congress, and I hope that I will have that. [But] like my predecessors of both parties, I have not agreed that I was constitutionally mandated to get it."[8]

Then acting on another precedent established during the operation in Somalia, Mr. Clinton directed the troops to replace Haiti's leader and disarm the civilian population. In an age when precedents are swiftly relied on to justify additional action, the UN's newly adopted role of choosing national leaders and disarming civilians constitutes a threat to the independence of any nation, certainly including ours.

• **Hiding Funding for UN Operations.** The California Earthquake Relief Bill of February 13, 1994 supplied millions of dollars in aid for earthquake victims. But it also produced $1.2 billion for UN-approved U.S. military operations in Somalia, Bosnia, and elsewhere. Where were the "diligent" congressional watchdogs of the public purse?

• **Foreign UN Commanders Order U.S. Forces Into Combat.** In April 1994, a blue-helmeted British UN troop commander and a UN diplomat from Japan, acting with the enthusiastic concurrence of the Egyptian bureaucrat who serves as UN Secretary-General, ordered U.S. fighter planes from NATO to attack positions in Bosnia. General Sir Michael Rose, Yasushi Akashi, and Boutros Boutros-Ghali didn't bother to contact President

Clinton or Congress. And our commanders in the field promptly complied with the UN's order. Obviously, the UN had already been given authority to employ U.S. forces serving in NATO, a UN subsidiary. Another momentous precedent had been established.

• **U.S. Forces Training for "Peace Maneuvers."** In August 1994, the *Washington Post* reported from Fort Polk, Louisiana that U.S. Army units were engaged in exercises "made to resemble real-life peace enforcement operations." The article mentioned full-scale mock conditions in which an army unit had been assigned "to disarm the militia."[9]

• **Air Force Bases Designated for Global Operations.** On September 30, 1994, New Jersey's McGuire Air Force Base was named headquarters of the new Air Force East Coast Air Mobility Wing. Equipped with Starlifter cargo jets and Extender refuelers, the base will be responsible for projecting U.S. military power throughout Europe and the East. Travis Air Force Base in California, with responsibilities in the Pacific region, had earlier been designated as headquarters for the West Coast Air Mobility Wing. The two bases will help to fulfill whatever UN-related missions a President assigns our forces.

As Air Force Chief of Staff nominee, General Ronald R. Fogelman (CFR) visited the McGuire base and, while referring to his Air Force command insignia, stated: "I wake up some mornings and I look at this patch and I wonder whether it is the United States command or the United Nations command." He was then sworn in as Air Force Chief of Staff and a member of the Joint Chiefs of Staff in the Pentagon.[10]

• **Troops to Rescue UN Force from Bosnia Quagmire.** In December 1994, President Clinton offered to send 25,000 U.S. troops to war-torn Bosnia to assist with the withdrawal of UN peacekeeping forces. The UN force of approximately 23,000 troops, 8,000 vehicles, and thousands of tons of supplies had completely failed to defuse the civil war that had raged for several years.[11] Placing American forces in the middle of this centuries-old struggle for any reason whatsoever openly invites retaliation from either side and threatens to drag America into another conflict where there is no constitutional authorization for involvement. But it seems as though we have arrived at a point where whenever the UN calls for our troops, our nation's leaders respond.

• **Troops Assigned to Get UN Force out of Somalia.** On December 16, 1994, the Clinton Administration announced that several thousand U.S. Marines would be sent back into Somalia to help evacuate the remaining UN peacekeepers and remove the U.S. military equipment left behind when most of the U.S. troops pulled out over a year earlier. Senator Dan Coats (R-IN) protested, saying: "The original American withdrawal was prompted by a congressional mandate.... Not one U.S. soldier should be required to set foot on to Somali soil."[12]

• **UN Leader Proposes a "Rapid Reaction Force."** On January 3, 1995, UN Secretary-General Boutros-Ghali released a "Supplement" to his 1992 *An Agenda For Peace* as part of his contribution to the 50th anniversary celebration of the UN. The document contained his "conclusion" that the UN must have a "rapid reaction force ... for deployment when there was an emergency need for peace-keeping troops." He suggested that a number of countries form "battalion-sized units" to be available on call as "the Security Council's strategic reserve."[13]

Misuse of Military Invites UN Intervention Here

Does any of this fit the real purpose of our military? Is this why Americans put on the uniforms of our armed services? Is it for these type missions that the people of the United States allow themselves to be taxed hundreds of billions of dollars each year? Even more, could these newly assumed UN powers — employed with the obvious approval of some U.S. leaders — ever be wielded against the people of this nation?

On October 22, 1993, Washington DC Mayor Sharon Pratt Kelly found President Clinton unwilling to respond affirmatively to her request that he assign National Guard troops to patrol streets in her crime-ridden city.[14] Earlier that month, she may have seen an Associated Press report from the American territory of Puerto Rico noting that, for the first time in the history of our nation, American military units "have been pressed into routine crime-fighting service with police."[15]

If National Guard troops can be used for such a purpose, why not regular army units? Why not anywhere in the nation? Why not have the military supplant local control of police and usher in a police state? Why not have foreign troops under UN auspices brought here to do the job?

One month before Mayor Kelly's request for troops, *Chicago Tribune* columnist Bob Greene suggested that it was time to consider stationing a UN multinational force here in the United States "to help bring tranquility and safety" to our streets. While American forces are scattered all over the world in UN missions and in defense of other nations, here is an implied call for UN-directed foreign troops to patrol our cities.[16]

On March 29, 1994, the *Los Angeles Times* published an op-ed column claiming, "It's time to send the Army into our cities to restore order, to disarm dangerous populations, and to detain those who are causing their neighbors to live in fear." Catherine O'Neill, co-founder of the Women's Commission for Refugee Women and Children, asked why troops should be sent "to restore order in Mogadishu" when they could be used to "get control of our neighborhoods."[17]

In May 1994, Clinton Administration officials agreed to participate in a UN study whose objective is to establish international controls over the manufacture and sale of handguns to civilians. The planned controls are aimed at the United States and other free nations. If the UN can use U.S. troops to disarm civilians in Somalia and Haiti, a precedent has been set for the UN to use troops from elsewhere to disarm any nation, including ours. U.S. leaders plan to have our nation represented at the Spring 1995 UN conferences dealing with this proposal.[18]

The enemies of freedom within the borders of the United States continue to take steps toward the creation of their new world order.

Summing Up

Over the past few years, leaders of this nation have led the way in helping to beef up the UN, expand its role, create precedents for future frightening uses of UN power, and place our nation's military at the service of the world organization.

U.S. leaders now acquiesce in the UN's newly proclaimed power to use military force (mostly supplied by this nation) to:

• Override the UN Charter and intervene in matters which are essentially within the jurisdiction of any nation.

• Replace national leaders.

• Disarm civilian populations.

• Engage in "nation building."

• Launch humanitarian missions that can be converted to other purposes once troops are on the scene.

These same national leaders allow the placement of American forces in UN missions under foreign commanders, and give individuals from other nations authority to commit our forces to military action.

As all of this unfolds, America's top officials ignore the U.S. Constitution as if it didn't exist and supply the UN with military forces, equipment, and funding to carry out its newly proclaimed missions.

Our Presidents and congressional leaders act as they do because they are obviously committed, not to the nation they are supposed to serve, but to the UN. They are working for a UN-directed "new world order," not an independent United States. Their increasingly bold agenda indicts them as agents of a conspiracy.

To say that America needs better leaders is to state the obvious. The only sensible course for our nation is to get out of the UN, a goal increasingly desired by the American people — but the exact opposite choice of America's current leaders.

The UN may not have succeeded in all of its operations, and it hasn't achieved the world dominance sought for it. But it has been given a series of menacing precedents it can use at any time in the future. Time is running out for nations that want to be sovereign and peoples who want to be free.

The alarm bells we are issuing won't be of any value if the plans of the UN and its promoters aren't soon thwarted. And so we direct these warnings to fellow Americans — who still have the capability of changing the course of history away from a future marked by UN tyranny and back to a truly independent and free America.

How to do it? A major step in that direction can be achieved by forcing those who lead this nation to abide by their oath to the U.S. Constitution. Its limitations regarding the President's power to make war and use the armed forces, as well as the usurpation of power recent Presidents have taken, are examined in the next two chapters.

Chapter 4

The Constitution Authorizes an Army and a Navy

The Congress shall have power ...

To raise and support armies, but no appropriation of money to that use shall be for a longer term than two years:

To provide and maintain a navy....

— U.S. Constitution, Article I, Section 8

As can be seen from the Constitution's actual text, the grants of power to Congress to create an army and a navy appear separately and are given with different wording. Congress may "raise and support" armies, but may not appropriate funds to maintain them for "a longer term than two years." But there is no funding limitation regarding the grant of power to "provide and maintain" a navy. In addition, unlike the permission to establish an army, there is an implied mandate that a navy must be created. Why the difference?

Because we know that the men who wrote the Constitution considered the wording of each clause very carefully, there have to be sound reasons for this dissimilarity. The difference, in general, is that the Founders believed the navy to be a permanent necessity, but an army only an occasional requirement that could well become a dangerous instrument in the hands of an unscrupulous leader.

The navy, said Madison in *Federalist* #41, "will be a principal source of her security against danger from abroad," and will be a force "such as can never be turned by a perfidious government against our liberties." A navy would also help to guarantee the safe conduct of our own nation's commerce among the nations.

History As a Guide

Eleven years before the Constitutional Convention of 1787, the Declaration of Independence spelled out why our nation was created and why there was strong sentiment to break away from Britain. In part the United States of America was born, the Declaration proclaimed, because King George had "kept among us, in Times of Peace, Standing Armies, without the Consent of our Legislatures." He had also "affected to render the Military independent of and superior to the Civil Power."

The attitude of the 56 who signed the Declaration of Independence was certainly shared by George Washington and the 38 others who put their names to the Constitution. (There were only four men who signed both documents.)

Their extensive knowledge of history convinced the Founders that the very existence of a standing army during peacetime posed a danger from within. Hence, in explaining what the 1787 convention had stated, Madison mentioned the possibility that "a perfidious government" might eventually come to power and use available military might to destroy liberty. He explained in *Federalist* #41:

> Not the less true is it that the liberties of Rome proved the final victim to her military triumphs; and that the liberties of Europe, as far as they ever existed, have, with few exceptions, been the price of her military establishments. A standing force, therefore, is a dangerous, at the same time that it may be a necessary, provision. On the smallest scale it has its inconveniences. On an extensive scale its consequences may be fatal. On any scale it is an object of laudable circumspection and precaution.

In this same essay, Madison pointed to 15th century Europe for examples of harm done to peoples whose nations maintained military establishments during times of peace. He pointed out that these forces were frequently used by rulers against some foreign nation in a contrived war or even against the people themselves.

Holding that there was no essential need for a *permanent* army in the new nation ("The Union itself destroys every pretext for a military establishment..."), the man who became our nation's fourth President cautioned that creating one could result in "liberty everywhere crushed between standing armies and perpetual taxes."

Madison was certainly not a pacifist. Nor were his colleagues at the Constitutional Convention. But fear of the potential misuse of a standing army was widespread amongst them. In *Federalist* #8, Alexander Hamilton expressed one element of this concern: "It is of the nature of war to increase the executive at the expense of the legislative authority." Hamilton feared giving the leader of our nation a permanent army that could be used to build the power of government over the people.

Would any American leader ever lead this nation into war in order to expand his own power over both the people and the other branches of government? Would any American leader contrive with the leader of a foreign power to have their nations go to war in order to build power for themselves? History confirms that the use of such tactics has often plagued mankind. Four centuries before Christ, Plato warned in *The Republic*:

> When the tyrant has disposed of foreign enemies by conquest or treaty, and there is nothing to fear from them, then he is always stirring up some war or other, in order that the people may require a leader.

War always results in more government and less personal freedom. It can even be the catalyst for building world government to dominate both nations and peoples. Hamilton noted in *Federalist* #8:

> Safety from external danger is the most powerful director of national conduct. Even the ardent love of liberty will, after a time, give way to its dictates. The violent destruction of life and property incident to war, the continual effort and alarm attendant on a state of

> continual danger, will compel nations the most attached to liberty to resort for repose and security to institutions which have a tendency to destroy their civil and political rights. *To be more safe, they at length become willing to run the risk of being less free.* [Emphasis added.]

In 1904, the potential harm from military establishments caught the attention of the authors of a volume entitled *Centennial of the United States Military at West Point*. In their comprehensive discussion of America's military history, they noted that, even before the 1787 Constitutional Convention,

> Congress indicated its feelings by declaring that "standing armies in time of peace are inconsistent with the principles of republican government, dangerous to the liberties of a free people, and generally converted into destructive engines for establishing despotism.[1]

Stephen Ambrose's 1966 book *Duty, Honor, Country: A History of West Point* referenced the October 1939 issue of *The Classical Journal,* in which historian Charles F. Mullett pointed out that many of the early American writers based their calls for independence on their knowledge that "the threat of the sword to … liberty had been constantly revealed by Roman history."

Need Triumphs Over Fear

While Hamilton expressed many misgivings about the existence of a standing army, he nevertheless agreed that permanently barring one would be foolhardy. In *Federalist* #25, he wrote:

> If … it should be resolved to extend the prohibition to the *raising* of armies in time of peace, the United States would then exhibit the most extraordinary spectacle which the world has yet seen — that of a nation incapacitated by its Constitution to prepare for defense before it was actually invaded.... We must receive the blow before we could even prepare to return it. All that kind of policy by which

> nations anticipate distant danger and meet the gathering storm must be abstained from, as contrary to the genuine maxims of a free government. We must expose our property and liberty to the mercy of foreign invaders and invite them by our weakness to seize the naked and defenseless prey, because we are afraid that rulers, created by our choice, dependent on our will, might endanger that liberty by an abuse of the means necessary to its preservation.

Having stated his own fears about the potential for danger in any standing army, Madison agreed to the creation of one, but with an important control added. In *Federalist* #41, he stated: "Next to the effectual establishment of the Union, the best possible precaution against danger from standing armies is a limitation of the term for which revenue may be appropriated for their support."

As a result, the Constitution didn't bar the formation of an army during peacetime. And it granted power to create such a force, not to the President, but to Congress. Further, it required Congress regularly to rethink the wisdom of maintaining such an army by specifying that no appropriation for its continued existence "shall be for a longer term than two years." In other words, if Congress saw danger arising from the army it had called into being, it could simply abolish it by withdrawing funds.

Joseph Story served as a justice of the Supreme Court in the early 1800s. Widely regarded for his scholarship, Story authored numerous dissertations about the meaning of the Constitution. In his two-volume *Commentaries on the Constitution* published in 1858 after his death, we find:

> In England, the King possessed the power of raising armies in the time of peace according to his own good pleasure. And this prerogative was justly esteemed dangerous to the public liberties. Upon the revolution of 1688, Parliament wisely insisted upon a bill of rights, which should furnish an adequate security for the future. But how was this done? Not by prohibiting standing armies altogether in time of peace; but by prohibiting them *without the consent of Parliament*. This is the very proposition contained in the Consti-

> tution; for Congress can alone raise armies; and may put them down, whenever they choose.

The Constitution also grants Congress power to "provide for calling forth the militia to execute the laws of the union, suppress insurrections, and repel invasions." Again, this power wasn't given to the President, but to Congress, one body of which (the House of Representatives) was to represent the interests of the people, and the other body (the Senate prior to the 17th Amendment's requirement for direct election of its members) the interests of the states.

What About Today?

More than 200 years since the Constitution became the supreme law of the land, concern about the misuse of our nation's military by Congress or the President is nowhere near that expressed by the Founders. As we have seen, the fear of the men at the Constitutional Convention centered around the potential that an unscrupulous leader might turn military forces at his disposal against the people and their liberties. They knew that ambitious and power-craving leaders had done so throughout history.

But never in their wildest nightmares did the founders imagine the use of our armed forces as a vehicle for building world government. Today there are good reasons to recall the fears our Founding Fathers expressed in the 1780s. But there should additionally be even greater apprehension about the actual use of our military as an instrument to build the United Nations.

It would be horrible enough if, in attempting to remain safe from external danger, the American people allowed their own leaders to build a military establishment and use it to compromise the people's liberties and squander their wealth. It is even worse, however, to discover that the people's innate yearning for safety — allowing our government to maintain a powerful standing army — is now providing unscrupulous leaders with the means to use these forces to enslave Americans and all the world through global government. Yet, this is precisely what is happening.

But the Constitution places additional limits on the misuse of the military. Even though it designates the President as Commander in Chief of the military, it grants Congress exclusive power to declare war. In the next chapter we analyze these additional portions of the Constitution and show how they, too, are being ignored or misused.

CHAPTER 5

Congress, the President, the Military, and the Constitution

The Congress shall have Power ... To declare War....
— U.S. Constitution, Article I, Section 8

So clearly did the Constitution grant to Congress alone the power to declare war that the matter is barely mentioned in any of the essays that make up *The Federalist Papers*. There simply wasn't any need to explain what was obvious.

James Madison addressed the possibility that war might have to be declared, but he said nothing about where the power to do so lay. In *Federalist* #41, he stated that the very first power granted to the government had as its object "security against foreign danger." And he added: "Is the power of declaring war necessary? No man will answer this question in the negative. It would be superfluous, therefore, to enter into a proof of the affirmative."

After participating in the Constitutional Convention, Charles Pinckney went home to South Carolina to take part in his state's ratification convention. Jonathan Elliot's massive collection of the statements of participants in the various state conventions claims of Pinckney that he "Observed that the President's powers did not permit him to declare war."[1] Thomas Jefferson commented briefly about the power of Congress to declare war: "The question of declaring war is the function equally of both houses [of Congress]."[2]

Other than these few references, little was stated by the Founders concerning the congressional power to declare war. It was clear to them that the President alone could not involve the nation in war.

But we are now 200 years since the adoption of the Constitution. During the Korean War (1950-53), a precedent was set — and then later appealed to — whereby Presidents send our armed forces into war without receiving the required declaration of the Congress.

The Presidents who arranged such a startling transfer of congressional war-making power, and the members of Congress who allowed it to happen, are equally guilty of disregarding the document they are sworn to uphold. In addition, they share responsibility for the many lives lost and resources squandered in these undeclared wars. Because they also transferred much of our nation's jurisdiction over any subsequent American participation in war to the United Nations, they must also be held accountable for compromising a major element of national sovereignty.

The "Commander in Chief"

Article II, Section 2, Clause 1 of the Constitution states:

> The President shall be the commander in chief of the Army and Navy of the United States, and of the militia of the several States, when called into the actual service of the United States.

The very first matter to be understood about this article of the Constitution is that it *constitutes an assignment of responsibility, not a grant of power*. The Founders had no intention whatsoever of giving the President power to employ any portion of the military for purposes beyond defending the lives and property of the people and the territory of this nation.

In *Federalist* #69, Hamilton made clear his understanding that a President acting as Commander in Chief is "nothing more than ... first general and admiral of the Confederacy." About the power to command the militia, he wrote in this same essay: "The President will have only the occasional command of such part of the militia of the nation as by legislative provision may be called into the actual service of the union...."

In *Federalist* #74, Hamilton discussed another reason for the designation of Commander in Chief:

> Of all the cares or concerns of government, the direction of war most peculiarly demands those qualities which distinguish the exercise of power by a single hand. The direction of war implies the direction of the common strength; and the power of directing and employing the common strength forms a usual and essential part in the definition of the executive authority.

The importance of civilian control over the military is also implicit in the designation of the President as Commander in Chief. But perhaps the most weighty ingredient of the President's role as Commander in Chief is his power to "repel sudden attacks" with the military forces at his disposal. We know of no one who denies that this power exists. But that such power is limited, and that it therefore can be and has been abused, is without question.

James Madison and Massachusetts delegate Elbridge Gerry are each credited with forcing consideration by the Constitutional Convention of the following: "Moved to insert 'declare,' striking out 'make' war, leaving to the executive the power to repel sudden attacks."[3]

Therefore, the strict limitations on the power to declare war does not, as James Madison and Elbridge Gerry noted, take away from the President the power to commit our nation's forces in response to an emergency. If American territory, or the lives or property of our people, are attacked, waiting for Congress to meet, debate, and vote about the wisdom of retaliatory military action would likely result in more lost lives and property, and even encourage further attacks.

On October 7, 1993, the Congressional Research Service of the Library of Congress issued a report to Congress entitled "Instances of Use of United States Armed Forces Abroad, 1798-1993."[4] The report lists 234 instances in which our military was employed outside this nation. Of the 234 cases listed, only five resulted from congressional declarations of war.

The report demonstrates that during the first 150 years of our nation's existence, these missions were created in response to acts of piracy or to protect American lives and property somewhere other than on the high seas. But it also shows that, ever since World War II and the creation of the United Nations, America's military forces have been used in behalf of other nations, other peoples, and other interests.

These uses include training the military of other nations, defending other nations against threatened invasions, assisting in various UN operations, aiding another nation's anti-drug operations, helping national leaders put down coup attempts, policing "no-fly" zones, etc. None of this use of our military was ever envisioned by Madison or any of the other Founders.

Illicit Uses of War

Commenting on the grant of war-making power to Congress and to Congress alone, Abraham Lincoln stated in a letter to law partner William Herndon:

> Allow the President to invade a neighboring nation, whenever he shall deem it necessary to repel an invasion, and you allow him to do so, whenever he may choose to say he deems it necessary for such purpose — and you allow him to make war at pleasure. The provision of the Constitution giving the war-making power to Congress was dictated, as I understand it, by the following reasons.... Kings had always been involving and impoverishing their people in wars, pretending generally, if not always, that the good of the people was the object. This, our Convention understood to be the most oppressive of all Kingly oppressions; and they resolved so to frame the Constitution that no one man should hold the power of bringing the oppression upon us.[5]

As Lincoln stated, our nation's Founders were cognizant of the possibility that a corrupt leader would engage the nation in wars calculated to enhance executive power and strengthen his control over the people. They knew full well that the kings of history had even created war as a way to abuse hapless subjects and to increase their own personal authority and wealth. Therefore, the power to raise an army was granted to Congress alone. In addition, the sole power to declare war was placed in Congress, where the representatives of both the people and the states could be found. There was to be no illicit use of war by any President!

Could there ever be such an abuse? Even with the Constitution's several limitations in mind, Hamilton still addressed the possible misuse of a standing army by an evil leader. In *Federalist* #25, he noted that because of the Constitution's safeguards, "a combination between the executive and legislative in some scheme of usurpation" would have to be created if it were ever to occur here. Looking into the future, he added:

> Should this at any time happen, how easy would it be to fabricate pretenses of approaching danger? Indian hostilities, instigated by Spain or Britain, would always be at hand. Provocations to produce the desired appearances might even be given to some foreign power....

In *Federalist* #26, Hamilton further addressed the potential for leaders to employ a standing force illicitly. He even speculated about the formation of a future "conspiracy" to subvert the liberties of an entire nation. Here are his words:

> An army, so large as seriously to menace those liberties, could only be formed by progressive augmentations; which would suppose not merely a temporary combination between the legislature and the executive, but a continued *conspiracy* for a series of time. Is it probable that such a combination would exist at all? Is it probable that it would be persevered in, and transmitted along through all the successive variations in a representative body, which biennial elections would naturally produce...? Is it presumable that every man the instant he took his seat in the national Senate or House of Representatives would commence a traitor to his constituents and to his country? Can it be supposed that there would not be found one man discerning enough to detect so atrocious a *conspiracy*, or bold or honest enough to apprise his constituents of their danger? [Emphasis added.]

Hamilton eventually concluded that his worries were ill-founded, that such a series of events as he described could never occur in this nation. He therefore agreed that it was both wise and proper for Congress to form an army for the common defense.

But Hamilton and the other Founders surely expected that the Constitution would always be understood and respected by the people and by their representatives in Congress. He could not imagine that powerful forces working in the shadows could arrange to have national leaders sell out their country to a world government.

Hamilton also never foresaw today's widespread abandonment of vigilance on the part of the people. He would be shocked to find that the fundamental principles he and others set so carefully in the Constitution's concrete are not taught in the schools, and are appreciated neither by the people in general nor by the nation's leaders who swear an oath to abide by them. He couldn't conceive of a time when elected officials would actually downgrade the worth of the Constitution and place far more importance on agendas concocted by their political leaders or, even worse, on commitments made to international pacts and agreements. And he would never have believed that the literal meaning of the Constitution would be superseded by radical interpretations issued by revolutionary justices of the federal courts.

Especially did Hamilton not foresee that a time would come when government officials in each branch would build on the people's fear of war in order to usurp their liberties and have them accept, not merely a despotic national government, but an oppressive world government.

War Powers Act of 1973

By 1973, after the nation had been sharply divided for years over the war in Vietnam, Congress finally asserted itself. If ever there was a case of closing the barn door after the horse had fled, it was the War Powers Act.

There was never any declaration of war authorizing the action in Vietnam. When the militant anti-war activists attracted sufficient attention, leaders in Congress introduced and gained passage of the War Powers Resolution.*

President Nixon vetoed the resolution, but Congress overrode his veto and enacted the measure into law. The Act stated that, in the absence of any declaration of war, the President is limited in his authority to involve troops in hostilities to 60 days, or, if he certifies a need for a time extension, to 90 days total. Further, the resolution gives Congress power to force the President to withdraw the troops from any such involvement whenever "the Congress so directs by concurrent resolution."

There has been no constitutional test of this measure and debate continues about its legality. The war in Vietnam ended before there was any attempt to invoke its provisions.

But congressional remedies to address improper uses of our nation's military forces already existed. Congress can cease funding for any misadventure begun by a President. And Congress can use its impeachment powers to remove a President who has assumed authority not granted to him by the Constitution.

Whatever may eventually be decided about the 1973 War Powers Act, it is regrettable that any member of Congress felt the need to enact it. But even though it has been enacted, it does not impede a President's clear authority to commit forces to repel sudden attacks, something that no one wants to cancel.

We shall marshal evidence in later chapters to show that the elements of the type of conspiracy imagined by Hamilton have indeed infected our nation. And we shall focus on the betrayal of our military as a major ingredient in the betrayal of America.

But first, we shall examine how changes in the military's ban on homosexuals is destroying our armed forces from within.

---

* The anti-war forces demanded that the U.S. pull out of Southeast Asia. Presidents Johnson and Nixon had been demanding adherence to their policy. The missing alternative, of course, was victory, something a parade of top military leaders claimed could have been achieved, not with ground war, but mainly by interdicting North Vietnam's supply routes.

Chapter 6

Inviting Homosexuals Invites Destruction

This is one of the few things I can think of that would strike at the core of faith within the infantry squad. To deny that is to deny human nature.

— Marine Corps Major Charles B. Johnson, as he resigned from the service after 17 years of duty, June 23, 1993

Bill Clinton was elected President of the United States on November 3, 1992. Eight days later, during a Veterans Day speech in Little Rock, he announced that he would lift the ban on homosexuals in the military as soon as he entered office the following January.

Various press reports noted in passing that the Clinton Administration plan represented the fulfillment of the President's promise to homosexual activists during the campaign. The President-elect was praised for being a man of his word and for keeping a firm commitment.

Paul Cellupica, a lawyer for the White House Office of National Drug Control Policy during the Bush Administration, still felt a need to remind Mr. Clinton of his pledge. In a November 7, 1992 *New York Times* op-ed piece, Cellupica trumpeted his own homosexuality while emphasizing the debt the new President owed to "gays":

> The Human Rights Campaign Fund, a national gay political-action organization, estimates that more than $3 million in gay political contributions were channeled to the Clinton campaign by various routes.

Homosexuals obviously believed they had a friend in Mr. Clinton. But the newly elected President was far more indebted to the millions of middle class Americans who expected him to keep his campaign pledge to work for an early cut in their taxes. And he additionally owed plenty to millions of labor union members who were given strong guarantees that he would protect their interests.

But the "early" tax cut never materialized. In its place, the President pushed hard and won congressional approval of the largest tax increase in the nation's history. Two years into his term, Mr. Clinton finally offered a patchwork tax cut in the aftermath of the political drubbing he and his Democratic Party received in the 1994 congressional elections.

Nor did it take long for Mr. Clinton to betray his labor union supporters. He thumbed his nose at their intense opposition to both the North American Free Trade Agreement (NAFTA) and the General Agreement on Tariffs and Trade (GATT). Actually, he showed who really commanded his loyalty when he put every ounce of his effort into backing these twin steps towards world government and the new world order.

The President's choices regarding NAFTA and GATT were either to 1) support labor's well-founded fears that the agreements would transfer jobs overseas, or 2) implement two major proposals advanced by internationalists and new world order advocates. As it turned out, he pushed to gain congressional approval of both pacts, proposals advanced by two organizations in which he has held membership: the Council on Foreign Relations and the Trilateral Commission.

A More Sinister Reason For Canceling the Ban

Delivering on his pledge to homosexuals, however, was practically the first item on Bill Clinton's agenda. For them, the military's ban constituted the last barrier to official national acceptance. Torie Osborn, executive director of the National Gay and Lesbian Task Force, would later mince no words in making this point:

> We have taken on the most conservative institution in America.... Down the line, we will get gay marriage. We're going to get the military to recognize us and our partners. We're going to promote our agenda. We're ready....[1]

Clinton handlers, however, conveyed the notion that he simply had to follow through on this firm promise, thereby deftly covering over a much more sinister purpose for overturning the 215-year-old ban. In addition to changing the national attitude toward homosexuality — which a change in the military policy would help accomplish — Mr. Clinton and other high Administration officials had to know they were undermining the character and make-up of our nation's military forces.

Lifting the ban on homosexuals has already begun to change the overall moral and principle-based attitude of the personnel who serve in the armed forces. Most who cannot accept such a fundamental change will depart; other potential soldiers will never enlist in the first place. The bulk of those remaining and many who will now be attracted to serve won't have the ethical standards any honorable nation wants in its military. Consequently, the new military will soon be staffed in large part by those who will accede to whatever radical alterations are demanded in their mission and command structure — like accepting the dictates of the United Nations.

In other words, welcoming homosexuals will make it far easier for our nation's leaders to gain acquiescence within the services for fundamental departures from past practices. Uniformed personnel who strongly adhere to the traditional reasons for the existence of our nation's armed forces, and who would fight to retain them, will be driven away.

Elsewhere in this book, we discuss the delivery of our nation's military forces to the United Nations. In chapter 10, we provide concrete evidence of the long-standing plans to disarm our armed forces and turn over all but a minuscule few personnel to an all-powerful UN "Peace Force" immune to challenge by anyone.

Would principled men who have taken seriously their sworn

oath to the U.S. Constitution stand for this? Would they passively accept a complete conversion of the military's role from serving our nation to serving the United Nations? The answer is perfectly clear: No, they would not. They would protest; they would even leave the uniformed services. But those who remain after the services are opened to homosexuals will find themselves serving in a military where they are expected to accept blindly any role given them.

It is also true that purging the services of the best men won't startle the American people; most won't know what's happening. It would, of course, be a great deal more difficult to hide from the people a mass of resignations, early retirements, and protests stemming from other concerns.

Good Men Are Resigning

When Marine Major Charles Johnson submitted his resignation in January 1993 in the wake of President Clinton's action, he gave several reasons for abandoning his 17-year career. (Married and the father of three youngsters, he left the service without the pension he would have been eligible to receive in less than three years.) He stated in his letter to superiors: "The new interim policy on homosexuals serving in the military constitutes an illegal order. I therefore tender my resignation at the government's earliest convenience." Illegal order? Isn't the President the Commander in Chief? Doesn't he have the authority to do what he did even if someone disagrees?

Major Johnson, who holds a PhD in policy analysis from Northwestern University and is a decorated combat veteran, chose his words carefully. He understands that the U.S. Constitution, to which both he and President Clinton have sworn allegiance, gives Congress alone the power to "make rules for the government and regulation of the land and naval forces."[2] If that means anything, it means that the President's January 29, 1993 order to the Secretary of Defense to draft "an Executive Order ending discrimination on the basis of sexual orientation" in the military constituted an intention to perform an illegal and unconstitutional act.

Johnson didn't rely totally on legality for his decision; he pointed to the harm that would flow from lifting the ban: "It has been proven in history that a battle is a function of a small unit, no bigger than a squad of about 13 men." He stressed that faith in others who will fight alongside and faith in one's superiors is critical. The policy change involving the ban on homosexuals, he claimed, "will cause unnecessary deaths in combat of soldiers, sailors and airmen." Referring specifically to his experience in the Marine Corps, he continued:

> When you breach that faith, you have broken the cohesion of the unit and degraded its effectiveness. When the small unit is less effective, more casualties, including deaths, result. This is one of the few things I can think of that would strike at the core of faith within the infantry squad. To deny that is to deny human nature.... The effects will be systemic.... It will destroy the Corps by our standards.

In a *Washington Times* article about Johnson's resignation,[3] reporter Michael Hedges related the attitude of other Marines about the Clinton directive. Former Marine Corps Commandant Robert Barrow, who retired in 1983, said that young officers with whom he had discussed the matter expressed "very nearly universal disapproval of homosexuals in military service within the Marine Corps." The former four-star general added: "I think this is one of the cruelest, most ill-advised, despicable acts perpetrated on an institution that has a certain purity to it." He hoped that it would not lead to mass resignations.

Hedges also noted that the January 1993 *Marine Corps Gazette* published an article carrying the startling title, "Disband the Marine Corps." Subtitled "It would be better to disband ... than see it dishonored and its virtues and values destroyed," Major Arthur J. Corbett's commentary stated, "The young officers who attempt to explain how homosexuality is an 'alternate' instead of a deviant lifestyle will quickly lose the respect of their Marines and a bit of their own honor in the process."

Destroying Unit Effectiveness

Men from all the services were equally outraged about Mr. Clinton's plans. Retired Army Colonel David Hackworth, our nation's most decorated living veteran, says, "I cannot think of a better way to destroy fighting spirit and gut U.S. combat effectiveness." Retired Rear Admiral J. Lloyd Abbot Jr. told a Mobile, Alabama gathering of Purple Heart recipients on February 6, 1993 that, because of the President's plan, "the armed forces of the United States face a greater crisis than any which they've faced since the nation was founded in 1776!"

Civilians familiar with the role of the military also spoke out. UCLA anthropologist Anna Simons spent 17 months studying the habits of a 70-man unit of the Army's Green Berets. In her opinion, removing the ban on homosexuals in the military would "destroy small-unit cohesion." Strongly doubting that the warrior bond could be maintained if open homosexuals were assigned to such a force, she argued, "You need to understand what being in combat is all about and then work that backwards before you begin your social engineering."[4]

Charles Moskos is a military sociologist at Northwestern University. He, too, contends that permitting homosexuals in the services will destroy combat effectiveness:

> We are asking men in combat to do an essentially irrational thing — put themselves in a position where they are likely to get killed.... One of the few ways to persuade men to do that is to appeal to their masculinity.... Just think about what it would mean to demasculinize combat. The effect on combat effectiveness might be catastrophic.[5]

In another *Marine Corps Gazette* article appearing in April 1993, Captain Mark E. Cantrell capably knocked down all of the phony issues employed by advocates of removing the ban. In "No Place For Homosexuals," Cantrell discussed the devastating loss of discipline, morale, unit cohesiveness, and *esprit de corps* sure to occur when professed homosexuals are permitted to serve. As to what will be lost, he cited a passage from a book about the Vietnam War entitled *Battle for Hue, Tet 1968*. Author Keith W. Nolan wrote:

> The "noble cause of freedom for South Vietnam" didn't propel a Marine to run through enemy fire to pull a wounded man to cover. A politician at home praising "our boys overseas" wasn't the reason a man would refuse evacuation to a safe hospital after one or two wounds. "Mom, dad, and apple pie" had only little to do with a grunt keeping his sense of balance in the midst of one of the ghastliest actions of the Vietnam War. What caused many of these things to happen in Hue was simple comradeship.
>
> There are few human experiences comparable to the camaraderie and brother-love of a Marine infantry unit in combat. It doesn't matter what your background is, what color your skin is, how much schooling you've had, how much money your father makes. All that matters are the men in your squad or platoon. The whole world revolves around helping them, trying to keep your *** and their ***** alive when the shooting starts. The Marine grunts slept in the same holes at night, suffered under the same broiling sun and freezing monsoon rains, slogged through the same muddy paddy fields, and fought the same enemy. And when it came to fighting, the individual Marine did his best because he couldn't let his buddies down. Nothing else mattered. This was true in World War II and Korea, and was true again here in Vietnam.

Does anyone really expect a continuation of that kind of performance when men are forced to serve alongside homosexuals?

Resistance Collapses

When the Clinton plan created a storm of protest, the President backed off slightly and agreed to study the matter further. In July 1993, the Senate Armed Services Committee, led by Senator Sam Nunn (D-GA), and the House Armed Services Committee, led by Representative Ron Dellums (D-CA), produced a measure containing a compromise acceptable to the President. Under the new legislation, the services are required to adhere to a "don't ask, don't tell, don't pursue" policy which, despite the strident cries of militant homosexuals that it is a cave-in to their enemies, is actually a huge victory for them.*

While a great deal more can be said about the deficiencies of the "don't ask, don't tell" policy, the assessment of Senator Malcolm Wallop (R-WY) is worth considering: "What [Mr. Clinton] has done is allow gays to be in the military and lie about it. That is typical of the '60s generation that Clinton represents, where there is no specific element of morality that is binding. It's a situational ethic, and frankly, I think it's the worst of all possible solutions."

What did the change demanded by Mr. Clinton replace? The main casualty is Department of Defense Directive 1332.14, under which the services had previously functioned. In part, it states:

> Homosexuality is incompatible with military service. The presence in the military environment of persons who engage in homosexual conduct or who, by their statements, demonstrate a propensity to engage in homosexual conduct, seriously impairs the accomplishment of the military mission. The presence of such members adversely affects the ability of the Military Services to maintain discipline, good order, and morale; to foster mutual trust and confidence among servicemembers; to ensure the integrity of the system of rank and command; to facilitate assignment and worldwide deployment of servicemembers who frequently must live and work under close conditions affording minimal privacy; to recruit and retain members of the Military Services; to maintain the public acceptability of military service; and to prevent breach of security.

---

* The full Congress approved the new policy as part of the Defense Authorization Act in September 1993. Congress could have refused to accept the Clinton plan. By not doing so, it shares the blame for the change and all of its harmful consequences. The military now operates under one set of rules in the unrevised Uniform Code of Military Justice, and under another conflicting set in the "don't ask, don't tell, don't pursue" policy initiated in 1993.

For more than 200 years, official policy held that "homosexuality is incompatible with military service." The Uniform Code of Military Justice (revised and repromulgated by Congress in 1956) contains what is called the "Sodomy Statute" (Article 125), which calls for a court martial for those who engage in sexual activity with someone of the same sex.

What does the "don't ask, don't tell" policy bring with it? New York University Law Professor Stephen Gillers offered:

> More than any institution in society, probably including the family, the military insists that its effectiveness demands loyalty to the organization above loyalty to self. If there is something amiss, you're supposed to speak up. If homosexuality or its practice is considered wrong, you're supposed to acknowledge it and others are supposed to expose you. This so-called compromise is dishonorable on its face.[6]

Writing in *Time* magazine, Michael Kramer claimed that the policy mandates duplicity — even among non-homosexuals — about a matter that strikes at the root of military effectiveness:

> "Don't ask, don't tell" shouldn't work because it is reprehensible, a first ever official codification of a policy that encourages concealing a fact deemed material to an institution's smooth functioning.... The law prohibits discrimination in part by respecting one's privacy, but in each case the rationale assumes that the "secret" (one's religion or political beliefs, for example) is immaterial for job performance.[7]

More destructiveness beyond what has been accomplished by this policy change is being acquired through the courts. The homosexuals are winning practically every battle. And the losers (besides the military) are national honor, national roots, and, unless the matter is soon reversed, the nation itself.

Basic Morality the Casualty

Ronald D. Ray, an attorney from Louisville, Kentucky, is a highly decorated Vietnam War combat veteran and a colonel in the U. S. Marine Corps Reserve. As a Deputy Assistant Secretary of Defense during the Reagan Administration, he served as a member of the 1992 Presidential Commission on the Assignment of Women in the Armed Forces as an opponent of women in combat.

Ray has also fought hard against dropping the military's ban on homosexuals. His impressively researched book *Military Necessity and Homosexuality* shows the historical place held by morality as the core of the military profession.[8] Ray quotes John Adams, who chaired the 1775 Marine Committee leading to the creation of the U.S. Navy. The man who later became our nation's second President wrote: "Republican governments could be supported only by pure Religion or Austere Morals. Public virtue cannot exist in a Nation without private Virtue, and public Virtue is the only Foundation of Republics."

In his 1775 work, *The Rules and Regulations of the Navy of the United Colonies*, Adams set standards which for more than 200 years have guided all the services:

> The commanders of all ships and vessels belonging to the thirteen United Colonies are strictly required to shew in themselves a good example of honor and virtue to their officers and men, and to be very vigilant in inspecting the behavior of all such men, and to discountenance and suppress all dissolute, immoral, and disorderly practices, and also such as are contrary to the rules of discipline and obedience, and to correct those who are guilty of the same, according to the usage of the sea.[9]

This foundation upon which our nation's military profession has been operating for two centuries has been cast aside. The consequences will be immense.

Who Will Serve?

Service in the U.S. military is not a right; it is a privilege. Because it is not a right, many are routinely excluded on any number of accounts, including height, weight, age, physical condition, even a failing score on an intelligence test. In the past, those who qualified to serve knew that they were about to experience a markedly different type of living and would be expected to comply with rules such as the Uniform Code of Military Justice.

But homosexuals have waged a campaign since at least 1972 to have their "lifestyle" protected as a civil right and to brand any ban on it as illegal discrimination. As we have tried to show, it has nothing to do with civil rights and is mostly a matter of morality.

But the ban also crosses into the area of proper discrimination, much like the discriminatory policy excluding those with debilitating limitations from the armed forces. It is discrimination directed at those whose conduct and attitude exhibit a preference for homosexuality. Why such discrimination? Because of the well-founded certainty that the presence of homosexuals in a fighting unit will destroy its cohesiveness, make it less effective, and cause it to become more prone to casualties. This certainly should end the discussion, but it does not.

If some citizens can be discriminated against for reasons of height, etc., it should be within reason to discriminate against others whose morality is deemed unacceptable and certain to jeopardize the well-being of others. But our nation has been taken down the road of moral relativism. Officially speaking, this nation no longer has a moral base. All branches of government, especially the courts, have been working for decades to destroy America's moral underpinnings. This departure from our past is as serious as any that can be imagined. And this is precisely what the homosexual movement has been aiming at for many years.

So we are left with the realization that anyone contemplating military service will face being forced into association with homosexuals. That means being thrown into remarkably close contact with people who are many thousands of times more likely to suffer from the deadly and highly contagious condition known as AIDS.

A study published the October 1991 issue of the *American Journal of Public Health* reported the findings of a medical investigation of the health records of male soldiers *before* they became

HIV-positive. It showed that these men had dramatically higher rates of syphilis, several types of hepatitis, enlargement of lymph nodes, pharyngitis, mononucleosis, and herpes. Is this the kind of atmosphere supposed to attract recruits?

In addition, it is no secret that many homosexual men regularly seek out young boys with whom to engage in pedophilia. Would any man knowingly bring his family to live in an area where he knows there will be homosexuals? Men with families will flee from such places. Young servicemen who look ahead to raising a family will surely shun military service.

Combat always means casualties, with the loss of blood and the need for blood transfusions. A wounded soldier might need a blood transfusion from a comrade, but what if the comrade is a homosexual carrying the AIDS virus? Another bloodied soldier might need immediate care, but will he get it if he is suspected of being a homosexual?

Ending the ban on homosexuality will dampen the desire of the very best of young Americans to serve. Traditional-minded parents will recommend other careers for their children. Clergymen will steer their followers away from pursuing a military career. As Ronald Ray has observed, "It would not be the first time in Christian history that military service became unacceptable for Christians." In the fourth century, St. Ambrose held that moral decline had overtaken the Roman Empire, especially in the military where service had already ceased to be regarded as a common obligation and was considered a form of servitude which everyone tried to evade.

In a July 4, 1994 *Washington Post* article about escalating problems faced by military recruiters, staff writer John F. Harris reported on a Pentagon admission that "recruit quality ... has slipped." Asked about the situation, Major General Kenneth W. Simpson, chief of the Army's recruiting command, attributed it to "a host of negative factors," and offered, "Our most experienced recruiters tell us that it has become more difficult to attract, contract and hold quality young people for service in the Army." Ending the ban on homosexuals is surely one reason for this problem.

Undermining Began Before Clinton

With his books, articles, legal briefs, and correspondence, Ronald Ray has fought hard to maintain the military's ban on homosexuals. He thought he had strategically placed allies but found, to his dismay, that men he counted on were "accommodators."

During his term as chairman of the Joint Chiefs of Staff in February 1992, General Colin Powell told the House Budget Committee that homosexual behavior is "inconsistent with maintaining good order and discipline." But in January 1993, he abandoned any pretense of moral leadership when he told midshipmen at the Naval Academy that if removing the ban "strikes at the heart of your moral beliefs, then you have to resign."[10] Several months before the Clinton election in November 1992, Powell told Ray personally of the "inevitability" of homosexuals being allowed to serve.[11]

On August 11, 1993, Powell's successor as Joint Chiefs chairman, General John Shalikashvili, praised the Clinton decision to lift the ban. Also asked by the press about women in service, he stated, "I feel great about women in the military."[12]

While serving as Vice President, Dan Quayle sought to defuse criticism from homosexuals about the Administration's supposed objections to their agenda. The *Louisville Courier-Journal* for September 9, 1992 reported him as saying to homosexuals: "Listen to what the President says and what I say, and more importantly watch what we do. We are the ones who have implemented a non-discrimination policy when it comes to gays and lesbians."[13]

On March 11, 1992, former Bush Administration White House Chief of Staff John Sununu stated on the *Phil Donahue Show* that under then-Secretary of Defense Dick Cheney, "efforts have been made to move in the right direction in terms of allowing homosexuals to have more responsible positions both in the civilian sector and the military sector."[14]

The harm that this ill-conceived and destructive change has already wrought is immense. Our nation's armed services are being transformed because of it. That Bill Clinton and others could be unaware of the consequences of their actions is simply impossible. What is being done dovetails with other plans involving the future use — and ultimate destruction — of our nation's military.

As we have noted, the cancellation of the military's ban on homosexuality wasn't done merely to keep a campaign promise, and it wasn't done solely because the President and his team see nothing essentially wrong with the homosexual lifestyle. It was done to emasculate the military, the same reason the services are now forced to place women in virtually all military assignments.

We examine this other attack on the professionalism of our nation's military — its feminization — in the next chapter.

Chapter 7

War Is No Place for Women

No woman, even as a volunteer, should have the right to go into combat simply because she desires to do so. It is not a question of what she wants or of her right. It is a matter of jeopardizing the lives of soldiers, who depend on all members of the team to do their full share, and of the right of every American citizen to have the strongest national defense possible to protect his and her freedom.

— Brigadier General Andrew J. Gatsis, U.S. Army (Ret.)
The New American, March 16, 1987

The feminization of our nation's military began long before Bill Clinton entered the White House. All of the service academies, for instance, were forced to admit women in 1976 during the Ford Administration. From then until today, many sensible barriers to placing women in every conceivable military assignment have been torn down.

As with the matter of homosexuality, the issue of women serving has, at its core, nothing to do with their supposed right to be in the services. Wearing the uniform of this nation shouldn't be considered a right, but a privilege. If the military can properly exclude some persons for not meeting standards for height, age, physical and mental abilities, etc., it can and should exclude for such a basic characteristic as gender. It is hardly necessary to point out that males and females are different.

Only tortured logic and a complete abandonment of good sense can challenge the many arguments we are about to offer for banning women from most military assignments. An even greater mountain of evidence beyond what we offer here can be assembled to show the folly of placing women alongside men in the armed services. But we are again dealing with policymaking driven by hidden intentions. Deliberate destructiveness, not folly, undergirds what is being done to the services, and to the men and women who serve.

Women Can Serve, But in Limited Roles

American women have served honorably and ably in the military for many years. During World War II, the WACS and WAVES filled numerous supporting roles, enabling men to fight more effectively. Women served in the medical corps, in supply and communications, and in other billets where their talents and energies could be put to work without compromising unit efficiency or well-being.

But even when women fill these roles, there have to be limitations. Retired Brigadier General Andrew Gatsis is a 36-year Army veteran, a graduate of West Point, and one of the most highly decorated officers ever to serve in our nation's armed forces. He wouldn't bar women from serving where they can perform. But he cautions that women cannot be counted on to fill many roles even in the combat-support category. In an article he wrote for the March 16, 1987 issue of *The New American*, he stated:

> I have personally seen female soldiers unable to lift heavy equipment such as ammunition, mechanic's tool sets, filled sandbags, food crates, or large camouflage nets. They could not move field range stoves, teletype machines, heavy generators, or big field desks. During field exercises, they had great trouble changing heavy truck tires, hitching trailers to the trucks, and carrying people on medical litters. They could not brake, steer, and drive trucks in rough terrain, put up cumbersome antennas, erect large bulky tents, construct ammunition bunkers, dig adequate latrines, or lift tackle off recovery vehicles.

When women aren't able to perform these tasks — all of which fall into the category of combat support — men have to pick up the slack, requiring them to do their own jobs and someone else's too. But, because women may have been assigned these positions, there are no extra men to pick up the slack. Therefore, unit efficiency suffers, morale deteriorates, and the essential work needed to support the front line troops doesn't get done.

Nor is this a problem only for ground forces. General Gatsis reported similar problems in the Navy, where all the heavy equipment is designed with men in mind:

> Paint, for example, is carried in five-gallon cans that weigh up to 95 pounds; food on ship is in heavy crates that women cannot lift; and high-pressure firefighting hoses and refueling lines in the Navy inventory have proved nearly impossible for women to handle properly. At Norfolk, the steel cables used to demagnetize the hulls of ships weigh four pounds per foot and extend up to 500 feet. Furthermore, when the ship is sinking or damaged from enemy fire and all is in pandemonium, everyone must be capable of giving meaningful manual physical assistance in emergency actions, such as launching heavy life boats. The last thing needed at this time is onlookers and part-time help getting in the way.

Military roles that can be filled capably by women are few and far between. Females should never be placed in billets where they will be expected to do a man's job, even if they volunteer.

Everyone Knows the Difference

What General Gatsis recounted isn't some new discovery; everyone involved knows that women can't do what men are expected to do. During our nation's first century and a half, demanding physical standards had to be met by those who served in the military. But now, these standards have been revised and downgraded, and separate standards have been put in place, to supply tortured justification for placing women in positions where they are, by their very nature, unable to perform acceptably.

In his explosive book, *Weak Link: The Feminization of the American Military*,[1] former infantry officer Brian Mitchell points out:

> All of the services have double standards for men and women on all the events of their regular physical fitness tests. Young male marines must perform at least three pull-ups to pass the test, but women marines must only hang from the bar with arms flexed for 16 seconds. In the Army, the youngest women are given an extra three minutes to complete a two-mile run. All of the services require men to perform more sit-ups than women, despite the much-vaunted strength of the female midsection.

Mitchell and others have pointed out that, on average, women have barely half the upper body strength of men and two-thirds of the endurance needed to slog through muddy terrain with heavy packs. Numerous studies have concluded that the service academies have lowered their standards, or established separate standards for women. If women can't run in boots while carrying rifles, everyone runs in sneakers. If women can't get through the obstacle course, the course is changed. This is the way "equality" is arrived at for female cadets and midshipmen at our nation's military academies.

No one can deny these differences in physical capabilities. Yet, all of this and more has been brushed aside as if it simply doesn't exist. The military is being forced to accept a lie, and it has caused nothing but problems. Americans should be asking why.

The Military's Purpose

A nation has a military force for one reason, to fight and win a war. The armed services haven't been formed to engage in social experimentation, provide employment, or train individuals for jobs they might secure after serving. The military exists to guard the nation's safety and to fight to maintain it. Fight! Win! Stay Free! Any nation still possessed of its senses will send the most capable persons to accomplish this goal, and that excludes women. Adversaries will undoubtedly send their best, their physically strongest, and their most psychologically able to kill. How will America fare if we send our women and an enemy sends its men?

General Douglas MacArthur's final visit to West Point afforded him the opportunity to address the corps of cadets one last time. He had graduated from the academy many years before, and had even served as its superintendent. His love for "the long gray line" and for those who formed it was legendary. In his famous "Duty, Honor, Country" speech of May 12, 1962, he told the future officers:

> ... your mission remains fixed, determined, inviolable — it is to win our wars. Everything else in your professional career is but a corollary to this vital dedication. All other public purposes, all other public projects, all other public needs, great or small, will find others for their accomplishment; but you are the ones who are trained to fight; yours is the profession of arms — the will to win, the sure knowledge that in war there is no substitute for victory; that if you lose, the nation will be destroyed....

MacArthur died in 1964 and was spared seeing West Point opened to women. He didn't oppose women serving in the armed forces. But he knew that West Point and its sister service academies exist for the sole purpose of creating the world's finest combat-ready officers, the men who are privileged to receive the training needed to lead other men in the arduous task of winning wars.

When the debate raged in Congress over the proposal to open our nation's military academies to women, Congressman Larry McDonald (D-GA) implored his colleagues to realize that the academies exist solely to prepare young people for combat. "Let women who wish to serve in the military," he stated, "enter the several branches through one of the many other routes available to them. But they should never be placed in combat and, therefore, they should never take a place in the institutions created to train officers for combat. Each one allowed to enter will mean one less man receiving the training needed to win our wars."

In her monthly report for September 1989, Eagle Forum President Phyllis Schlafly, recalling Douglas MacArthur's West Point speech, expressed her outrage over the announcement that the position of first captain of the academy's corps of cadets had, for the first time, been awarded to a woman. A *New York Times* account of the selection attempted to reassure anyone who knew the academy's real mission by telling readers that this young lady possessed "a strong academic record, played soccer and competed in cross-country skiing ... and worked as a speech-writer at the Pentagon."

Schlafly recounted how, in his famous speech, General MacArthur had reminded the future army officers that combat was extremely demanding. The picture he painted for them included

> ... bending under soggy packs, on many a weary march from dripping dusk to drizzling dawn, slogging ankle deep through the mire of shell-shocked roads, to form grimly for the attack, blue-lipped, covered with sludge and mud, chilled by the wind and rain, driving home to their objective ... the filth of murky foxholes, the stench of ghostly trenches, the slime of dripping dugouts; those broiling suns of relentless heat, those torrential rains of devastating storm, the loneliness and utter desolation of jungle trails, the bitterness of long separation from those they loved and cherished, the deadly pestilence of tropical disease, the horror of stricken areas of war....

But West Point had chosen a 20-year-old girl to lead 4,400 cadets. Schlafly asked, "Can we believe that this 112-pound, 5-foot-4-inch girl can do that — and, in addition, lead troops of men to risk death under such circumstances? You have to be kidding!"

Psychological Differences

While physical differences surely militate against placing women in combat, psychological differences supply additional reasons for keeping them away from war. The most pronounced characteristic of combat is violence. General Gatsis maintained that "violence calls for force and force calls for physical strength." But it also calls for something that women don't have: the combination of combativeness and aggressiveness found in men. Of women, the general remarked, "They just don't like to beat up on people." He added:

> Our soldiers are taught out of necessity to be brutal and to kill. Like it or not, these are the talents that win battles. It is immoral to place our daughters in this role that they are not psychologically equipped to fill. Women are essential in the procreation of life, not in its destruction. Our fighting men must be tough enough to defend us against our enemy and our women must provide the gentleness needed to rehabilitate them into good family members upon their return from battle.

Anyone who has served in the military, especially if he has seen combat, understands the importance of bonding. Training throughout the military stresses the need to rely on the men with whom you serve, and having them rely on you. Confronting the claims of women's libbers and others head-on, General Gatsis insisted that the strong "macho feeling among soldiers bonds them together and promotes heroism and self-sacrifice that logic or reason cannot explain."

Though most women possess numerous admirable traits, they don't have what is needed to create military bonding. The general continued, "They don't have the masculinity that a male warrior is proud of; this is the ingredient needed to maximize a soldier's ability to kill and win. In fact, soldiers are more afraid of what their companions will think of their ability to fight than they are of the enemy. This macho spirit prevails throughout all ranks. But it is ridiculous to expect to find it in women."

In his article "Women Can't Fight," Vietnam veteran James H. Webb Jr. wrote of the fundamental dissimilarity between the sexes.[2] Still, the lie claiming that there are no essential differences between males and females continues to be championed by fools and subversives. The harmful effect on our nation's military is immense.

Brian Mitchell noted in *Weak Link* that no one should downplay the effects of premenstrual syndrome on the behavior of women.

He cited expert medical testimony warning that many women "experience severe PMS-related symptoms, including incapacitating depression, suicidal thoughts, extreme mood swings, self-abuse, and violence." He added that only ten percent of premenopausal women have none of these PMS symptoms.

Mitchell recounted an incident in South Korea in 1976, during which tensions at the North-South border flared up and all units were ordered to stand in combat-ready alert. "As soon as it became clear that the alert was no ordinary training exercise," he related, "commanders throughout Korea were flooded with requests from female soldiers for transfers to the rear." When it was refused, "many women abandoned their posts near the border and headed south on their own.... Others had reported for duty with dependent children in tow, since their arrangements for childcare did not cover the event of war."

Just imagine what that did for unit morale!

In 1993, the Pentagon lifted its ban against women pilots flying combat missions. In October 1994, one the first women training for such an assignment, Navy Lieutenant Kara S. Hultgreen, lost control of her F-14 Tomcat as she was preparing to land it on the carrier *USS Abraham Lincoln*. She died in the mishap, blazing a trail for women in a place where women should never have been placed.

War Is for Men to Fight

Partisans for placing women in combat point to Israel's successful employment of females. But as Brian Mitchell pointed out in *Weak Link*, Israel abandoned the policy many years ago because it was found to hinder everything the military sought to accomplish. Israeli women are barred from posts where there is physical strain, exacting environmental conditions, and combat. They serve instead as clerks, nurses, and instructors.

Other advocates insist that women have just as much right to die for their country as men. Schlafly responded: "Dying for your country isn't the purpose of the armed services; their mission is to make enemy troops die for *their* country. Men are demonstrably better at that task than women." She could have added that placing women in combat will endanger those with whom they serve, causing both them and others to die needlessly for their country.

General Gatsis wishes that those who agitate for placing women in combat "could see it as I have." He wonders if they are prepared to have their daughters, wives, and sisters exposed to situations where they must fight an enemy soldier with a rifle butt and a bayonet, where they have to drag dead corpses of their comrades away from barbed wire, or where they might themselves be horribly mangled and trapped in a mine field no one can penetrate. Knowing fully how male prisoners of war have been mistreated, he wonders if those who would place women in the front lines have considered what fate awaits those who might be captured.

Beyond what the presence of women in combat would do to the military, our nation's entire system of values suffers when the status of women is brought down to the level of men. A well-ordered society is built around the family, and the family's anchor is the woman and mother. Caving in to the demands of some women who shun this role isn't the way to strengthen this nation; doing so weakens it. The best of men understand this clearly and willingly accept their role as the protector of women. This is why men throughout history have volunteered to put on a uniform — to make the world a safe place for their women and children. It is incomprehensible that any real man would send a woman to do his nation's fighting.

There have even been some who claim that placing women in the ranks will inject a needed element of "refinement" into the services. Experience suggests exactly the opposite because men will fight over the women, will abuse the women, and will learn to despise them when they are unable to carry their share of the load.

All of this demonstrates the importance of keeping women out of combat and combat-support roles. But, in the name of equal opportunity, the U.S. military continues its feminization. The destructiveness brought on by such a policy is something those who have mandated this madness surely comprehend. They can't miss it because it jumps off every page and screams with every lowering of standards.

There is, therefore, the hidden motive, similar in effect to the one allowing homosexuals to serve. It is destruction of the military by forcing out of the services some of their best personnel, weakening the morale of those who remain, and giving our armed forces the task of building and maintaining unit cohesiveness where it simply can't be achieved. The ultimate goal is to have the services readily accept transfer to United Nations command for whatever the UN wants done anywhere on earth.

As we shall see in the next chapter, America has also suffered from long-range plans to create war and to build on predictable revulsion to its horrors. The goal of America's war-creators has been to destroy rock-solid determination of the people to maintain national independence and, ultimately, to gain their approval to take these United States into a world government.

Chapter 8

Creating War to Build Power and Destroy Freedom

But war's a game, which, were their subjects wise,
Kings would not play at.

— William Cowper, *The Winter Morning Walk*

England's William Cowper (1731-1800) was not the first to point out that kings have always been free to "play at" war because their subjects were unaware of the war's real purpose. The same has often been said of other leaders, in other ages, in other nations.

Earlier in these pages, we quoted Plato's warning about tyrants. He said they were "always stirring up some war," and were doing it for motives hidden from the people who had to fight it, and even pay for it.

William Shakespeare had King Henry IV advise his son, Prince Hal, "Be it thy course to busy giddy minds with foreign quarrels." The Bard of Avon knew that unscrupulous leaders throughout history have found that an easy route to increasing their power was to send their peoples to war.

In *Federalist* #26, Alexander Hamilton showed the same awareness when he worried about the misuse of military forces by a future President in "schemes to subvert the liberties of a great community."

And Abraham Lincoln applauded the absence in the Constitution of any presidential war-making power because "kings had always been involving and impoverishing their people in wars" for deceitful purposes. He was grateful that our Constitution barred any President from such kingly abuse.

In an article appearing in the February 10, 1946 issue of the *New York Times*, a man named David Low stated, "I have never met anybody who wasn't against war. Even Hitler and Mussolini were, according to themselves." The two leaders he mentioned, of course, led their nations into war. Like so many other tyrants and would-be tyrants, they were good at saying one thing and doing just the opposite. That practice continues to plague mankind.

Here in contemporary America, it is undoubtedly difficult for most to imagine that anyone, especially a fellow American, would work to create a war in order to further a secret agenda harmful to the people. Yet this is precisely what has been happening in our America throughout much of the 20th century.

In our country, however, the main motive of the warmakers has not only been to increase the size and reach of our government and their own personal power, but (in many cases) to create a world government to dominate all of mankind.

Norman Dodd and the Reece Committee

In 1953, a principled American named Norman Dodd accepted appointment as Research Director for the House of Representatives Special Committee to Investigate Tax-Exempt Foundations and Comparable Organizations. The purpose of the committee, spelled out in the House resolution creating it, was "to determine which such foundations and organizations are using their resources for un-American and subversive activities...."

The panel, chaired by Representative Carroll Reece (R-TN), decided at the outset to focus on the 12 largest American foundations (Carnegie, Ford, Rockefeller, and others) because they accounted for 70 percent of all foundation assets.

One of the committee's first moves was to send a formal inquiry to the groups to be investigated. Upon receiving his copy of the inquiry, Carnegie Endowment for International Peace (CEIP) president Joseph E. Johnson contacted Dodd by telephone and suggested that, instead of his answering all the questions, he would cooperate in having the committee send a staff member to foundation headquarters to examine the CEIP minute books.

Dodd accepted the offer at once and assigned the task to attorney Kathryn Casey, instructing her to focus on the decade 1910-1919. Returning from her assignment shocked and dazed, she reported to Dodd and he summarized her findings as follows:

> [In the minutes of the Carnegie Endowment for International Peace about 1911] the trustees raised a question. "Is there any means known to man more effective than war, assuming you wish to alter the life of an entire people?" [A]t the end of the year, they came to the conclusion that there was no more effective means to that end known to man. So, then they raised question number two, and the question was, "How do we involve the United States in a war?"[1]

Before he passed away, Dodd frequently recounted the shocking information his assistant found in those minutes. Available in a variety of sources traceable to Dodd and Miss Casey, these revelations supply forceful evidence showing that there were indeed solid reasons for Congress to undertake the investigation it had launched.

The Reece Committee's work was abruptly terminated in 1954. But Dodd had gathered enough data to conclude that the leaders of numerous large foundations had been using resources at their disposal to destroy the independence of the United States and create a world government ruled by themselves and like-minded individuals.

Several reasons why these men wanted to "alter the life" of the people in the United States come to mind. They sought to change the American people's desire to stay out of the affairs of other nations; they wanted to compromise, even destroy, our nation's independence; and their ultimate goal was to control all mankind through a world government they would establish. There was, of course, nothing patriotic in all of this; the motive was solely and entirely a grandiose and sinister grab for power.

At the mere mention of war, the ordinary mind conjures up thoughts of death, destruction, and hardship. But, as the trustees of the Carnegie Endowment well knew, war has its secondary effects. It certainly brings on more government. It spawns moral decline, provides an opportunity for government to redistribute wealth, and spreads a lessening of faith in a nation's institutions. War can also soften a people's character and induce them to give up their freedom. Because they wanted all of these consequences to befall our nation, these individuals wanted war.

Information gathered by the Reece Committee shows that wealthy and highly connected individuals at the apex of these foundations worked indefatigably to involve our nation in World War I. Similarly motivated persons subsequently involved the United States in newer and different types of war — e.g. Korea, Vietnam, Iraq — in order to move this nation steadily down the path toward world government and the new world order.

But we are jumping ahead to our conclusion. It is time to present some evidence to support what seems implausible.

Kathryn Casey's Further Discoveries

Kathryn Casey's work bared additional plans of the foundation's trustees. Norman Dodd also pointed to Miss Casey's further discovery that the trustees met in 1917 "and had the brashness to congratulate themselves on the wisdom of their original decision because already the impact of war had indicated it *would* alter life ... in this country." The trustees were so committed to having war change America that they even had the audacity, said Dodd, "to dispatch a telegram to Mr. Wilson, cautioning him to see that the war didn't end too quickly."

According to Dodd, Miss Casey also came upon information showing that these very same trustees later secured financial help from the Rockefeller, Guggenheim, and other foundations for two additional purposes: to gain influence over the State Department and to gain control over American education as a way of ensuring that "there would be no reversion to life in this country as it existed" prior to World War I.

What she learned during her stay at CEIP headquarters so disturbed Kathryn Casey that she was never again able to work effectively and, after being transferred to a low-level bureaucratic post and performing inadequately there, she ended up in a hospital for the mentally impaired.

America Into World War I

In 1916, while World War I was already raging in Europe, President Woodrow Wilson campaigned for re-election. Posters plastered all over the nation displayed his picture and the slogan, "He kept us out of war!" The horrible truth is that he and his key advisers — led by the ever-present Edward Mandell House and in keeping with the desires of the CEIP trustees — were planning to involve our nation in the war at the earliest possible moment. Even before the 1916 re-election campaign had begun, House traveled to England where he secretly committed the U.S. to the war.[2]

The Wilson Presidency was completely managed by House, the mysterious Texan who had befriended the former college president and New Jersey governor. Wilson biographer Charles Seymour points out in his four-volume work, *The Intimate Papers of Colonel House*, that Wilson said of his adviser, "He is my second personality. He is my independent self. His thoughts and mine are one."[3]

Part of the House-Wilson strategy called for spreading inflammatory propaganda throughout America about Germany's sinking of the British ocean liner *Lusitania* on May 15, 1915. Media and political campaigns successfully enraged the American people about Germany's attack on the supposedly "unarmed" passenger ship. Because there were many Americans among the 1,200 innocent passengers who perished, the people of this nation were led to the conviction that Germany should be punished.

But in his 1972 book, *The Lusitania*, British author and researcher Colin Simpson showed conclusively that the ship was a registered armed cruiser of the British fleet carrying military personnel and munitions, that it was sent unescorted into waters where German U-boats were known to be operating, and that it was actually a victim of deep intrigue emanating from both Washington and London. More than 50 years after the incident, this important book confirmed what many had suspected at the time of the tragedy.[4]

More than any single reason, Germany's sinking of this ship gave U.S. leaders an excuse to involve our nation in a war where we surely did not belong.

The American people were not told that Germany had tried unsuccessfully to purchase advertising space in numerous U.S. newspapers to warn prospective passengers that they would be endangering themselves by traveling in a ship known to be a man-of-war. Had those ads appeared, many would have abandoned plans to be aboard. And there was a great deal more that the peoples of this nation and England were not told about the incident, dubbed "a damned dirty business" by Lord Mersey, the head of the 1915 British inquiry.

Which means, of course, that 1,200 men, women, and children were sent to a watery grave so that America could be taken into a war that would prepare the American people for radical changes. Before World War I ended, 48,000 Americans were killed and 228,000 suffered wounds — all pawns in a vicious power play. Without doubt, some of the people behind the scenes who were directing this blood-drenched show wanted these deaths and maimings. Kathryn Casey, it should be recalled, had found the CEIP trustees urging President Wilson not to end the war "too quickly."

America actually entered the war in April 1917. On January 8, 1918, ten months before it ended, President Wilson delivered his famous "Fourteen Points" speech. In it, ever submissive to the prodding of Edward Mandell House, he proposed a world government organization known as the League of Nations. But the U.S. Senate rejected the idea in 1919. As indicated by the congressional elections of 1918, which resulted in strong gains for Republicans, plus the election of Republican William Harding as President in 1920, our nation was returning to "normalcy" despite having been dragged into World War I. From the point of view of the plotters, something more than the blood spilled in that war had to be arranged if world government were to become a reality.

The something more was arranged by Colonel House. Meeting with British counterparts while in Paris in 1919 to construct the Versailles Treaty at the end of the war, House and his team laid the groundwork for the formation of the Council on Foreign Relations. Formally launched in 1921, the CFR has drawn powerful and influential men and women into its net to work for the world government it has always sought. It quickly became and has remained the governing force behind the U.S. government. (See Appendix A.)

World War II Leads America Into the United Nations

In an eerie repeat of President Wilson's deceitful 1916 campaign performance, President Franklin Delano Roosevelt told the American people as he campaigned for reelection in 1940, "Your boys are not going to be sent into any foreign wars." But just as Wilson had done in his era, Roosevelt was lying. In his massively researched survey of the CFR's history and deeds, author James Perloff documents the steps taken by Roosevelt and his coterie of internationalist advisors from the CFR and elsewhere to goad Japan into attacking Pearl Harbor, and to insure that Germany declared war on the United States.[5]

The goal of President Roosevelt and his team was similar in many ways to what Wilson and House had sought two decades earlier: Push America into war and then induce the people to want and even clamor for world government. On July 10, 1941, five months before the U.S. entered the war, the President sent 80,000 American troops to Iceland to support the British forces stationed there. Because England and Germany were already at war, this move was widely viewed as our entry into the conflict through a back door. Senator Robert Taft (R-OH) immediately labeled the action unconstitutional, but Senator Tom Connally (D-TX) sprang to the President's defense and insisted that the action was proper. He cited numerous other instances where a President had deployed troops without congressional approval. But nothing like this troop deployment had ever been done before.

The President and General George Marshall then deliberately kept information about the impending Japanese attack on Pearl Harbor from military commanders in Hawaii. More than 2,000 Americans died in that raid, all sacrificed for a hidden purpose. Within days of the attack, Congress declared war on Japan and Germany declared war on our nation. America was now in another world war, this time on two fronts. The plotters had another glorious opportunity to "alter the life" of the American people.

When virtually everyone else was totally consumed with the war effort, world government planners immediately began taking concrete steps toward their ultimate goal. In 1942, delegates from the U.S. and 25 other nations met and issued a "Declaration of the United Nations," the first official use of the term "United Nations." In 1943, representatives of the USSR, Great Britain, Nationalist China, and the U.S. met in Cairo, Egypt, where plans were laid for the postwar creation of the world organization. In 1944, the initial drafts of the UN Charter were hammered out at a conference held at Dumbarton Oaks in Washington, DC.

Another high-level conference was held at Teheran, where Stalin was brought into the planning. Finally, after the allied leaders agreed at Yalta in February 1945 to form a world government organization, the UN's founding conference convened in San Francisco from April to June of 1945. The European phase of World War II ended in May 1945; Japan capitulated in August 1945. In the wake of all the misery of another war, the world was ready to try at the plotters' long-sought-after world government.

Plotters All Linked

At the San Francisco conference where the UN Charter was finalized, more than 40 of the U.S. delegates were or soon would become members of the Council on Foreign Relations. One of them, Carnegie Endowment for International Peace trustee James T. Shotwell, was a CEIP trustee who participated in that group's 1911 planning sessions where the trustees decided to use war as the means "to alter the life" of our nation. The CEIP president during the 1910-19 period was former Secretary of State Elihu Root. One of the earliest members of the CFR, he served from 1931 until his death in 1937 as its honorary president. Had he lived longer, he would surely have been amongst the U.S. delegates at the UN's founding conference.

The formal report issued by the Reece Committee made note of these organizational linkages. Congressman Reece stated:

> Miss Casey's report shows clearly the interlock between the Carnegie Endowment for International Peace, and some of its associated organizations, such as the Council on Foreign Relations and other foundations, with the State Department. Indeed, these foundations and organizations would not dream of denying this interlock. They proudly note it in reports. They have undertaken vital research projects for the Department; virtually created minor departments or groups within the Department for it; supplied advisors and executives from their ranks; fed a constant stream of personnel into the State Department trained by themselves or under programs which they have financed; and have had much to do with the formation of foreign policy both in principle and detail.
>
> They have, to a marked degree, acted as direct agents of the State Department. And they have engaged actively, and with the expenditure of enormous sums, in propagandizing ("educating"?) public opinion in support of the policies which they have helped to formulate....
>
> What we see here is a number of large foundations, primarily the Rockefeller Foundation, the Carnegie Corporation of New York, and the Carnegie Endowment for International Peace, using their enormous public funds to finance a one-sided approach to foreign policy and to promote it actively, among the public by propaganda, and in the government through infiltration. The power to do this comes out of the power of the vast funds employed.[6]

In addition to the dozens of CFR members involved in the UN's founding, 17 individuals were named by the State Department itself as having helped to shape U.S. policies leading to the creation of the UN. All but one were later identified as secret communists.[7]

The close relationships among these individuals from the CEIP, the State Department, the Communist Party, and the CFR — all of whom were working to create the UN — is typified by the career of Alger Hiss. From his position as a high official of our nation's State Department, he was named Secretary-General of the UN's founding conference and became its most important figure. The CFR welcomed him to membership in 1945. After the UN Charter had been accepted and the organization began to function, Hiss left the State Department in 1947 to become CEIP president. Then, in the celebrated espionage case ending in January 1950, Hiss was convicted of perjury for lying about his Communist Party membership which dated back to the 1930s.

Hiss was, therefore, a high State Department official, a secret Communist Party member, a CFR member, the Secretary-General of the UN's founding conference, and the president of the CEIP. Many other UN founders had most of these same credentials.*

The Carnegie Endowment wanted world government, was perfectly willing to propel our nation into war to get it, and has successfully penetrated the State Department and American education to promote its agenda. The Council on Foreign Relations, whose membership interlocked with the CEIP from its outset, and with the Communist Party during the 1940s, was brought into existence to propagandize Americans into wanting world government. Communists in our nation and throughout the world labored diligently to bring the UN into existence and to have it located in the United States.[8] And the UN, the beneficiary of all of this support, has worked throughout the years to undermine U.S. sovereignty and to destroy the freedoms enjoyed by the

---

* In 1941, the CEIP's annual *Yearbook* revealed that its economics and history division was planning for "a new world order." Subsequent editions of the *Yearbook* discussed the organization's close cooperation with the CFR and numerous other foundation-supported organizations in efforts to bring the UN into existence.

American people. As detailed above, Alger Hiss, a convicted traitor to the nation of his birth, provides a common thread through all five groups (State Department, CFR, Communist Party, CEIP, and UN).

A more current CEIP proposal, published in the Winter 1992/93 issue of the CFR's *Foreign Affairs*, called for "greater American support for both U.N. peacekeeping and peacemaking efforts." In its "Special Report: Policymaking for a New Era," the CEIP recommended the creation of a "major military command ... to support U.N. military operations and, if necessary, U.S. participation in them," and also the assignment of "one or two U.S.-based brigades for support of U.N. operations." This group hasn't changed its overall goal one iota.

Gaining U.S. Approval for the UN

Once the UN Charter had been completed, the major task confronting the world planners was to get the U.S. Senate to approve it. Great pressure from many quarters was brought to bear on the senators. From within their own ranks, pro-UN Senator Tom Connally (D-TX) told his colleagues, "The nations of the world remember how the League of Nations was slaughtered here on this floor." He and others high-handedly accused any opponent of U.S. entry into the League in 1919 of guilt for the widespread death and destruction of World War II.

But the main issue regarding U.S. entry into the UN should have been national sovereignty. If our nation joined the world organization, would we still control our own destiny? And, of fundamental importance, would our military forces remain under U.S. control?

On July 23, 1945, while the Senate was debating the matter, the rabidly pro-UN *New York Times* summarized the Truman Administration's position as follows:

> It is this administration's contention that if the Senate ratifies the Charter in the first stage, they accept a moral obligation to all other signatories of the San Francisco Charter to place at the dis-

> posal of the new organization an adequate supply of forces which will be available for use anywhere the Security Council, including the United States delegate, decides to send them, and without authorization of the Congress in each case.

That accurate statement should have been enough to convince senators to steer clear of the UN. But pro-UN Senator Arthur Vandenberg (R-MI) told his colleagues on July 24th: "We shall decide for ourselves where we wish to draw the line, if any, between the constitutional authority of the President to use our armed forces in preliminary national defense action and the constitutional authority of Congress to declare war." His inclusion of the phrase "if any" is significant. He was obviously willing to accept the notion that the President could assign troops for UN missions without congressional approval, but he couched his willingness in political jargon.

President Truman himself, while urging the Senate to ratify the treaty, addressed the key issue of troop deployment: "When any such agreement or agreements are negotiated, it will be my purpose to ask the Congress by appropriate legislation to approve them." Note that he did not say he was duty-bound to consult Congress. Here we had another politician delivering an empty promise he had no intention of keeping. Pro-UN Senator Paul Lucas (D-IL) joined in with assurance for his fellow senators that they had little to worry about because Mr. Truman's stand "eliminates any possibility that assignment of military contingents would be made without consulting Congress." The Truman stand did nothing of the kind.

Some of the traitors to our nation were quite open about what they intended. John Foster Dulles, a disciple of Edward Mandell House, a CFR founding member, a State Department functionary, and a delegate to the San Francisco conference, openly and enthusiastically supported empowering the United Nations to use our military forces. Dulles claimed that, once the U.S. had ratified the UN Charter, we had no right to restrict the world body's use of our troops.

Opposition Weak and Ineffective

Only a few voices were heard expressing fears that the UN would dominate our military and cancel several vital portions of the Constitution. That they were too few and totally overwhelmed by the mountains of support for the world body became plainly evident. The need for "peace" in the aftermath of a horrible world war was incessantly drummed into every American, and especially every senator.

One small bit of resistance came from Senator Burton Wheeler (D-MT). He worriedly spoke out on July 24th:

> [I]f we enter into this treaty, we take power away from the Congress, and the President can send troops all over the world to fight battles everywhere. If you say that is the policy of this country, I say the American people will never support any senator or representative who advocates that policy, and do not make any mistake about it.

Four days later, however, even Wheeler cast his vote for the Charter, expecting that he would be able to take a stand about delivering troops to the UN whenever the President asked Congress to approve such a move. As is now known from the many instances when troops have been dispatched to the far corners of the earth, congressional approval has occasionally been sought, but never for a declaration of war.

Also on July 24th, an editorial appearing simultaneously in the *New York News* and the *Washington Times-Herald* attacked the pro-UN position: "This United Nations Charter embodies Roosevelt's dreams of a post-war super-state. It entails the destruction of parts of the written Constitution without a by-your-leave to the American people." Precisely!

Senator Henrik Shipstead (R-MN), one of the two senators who opposed ratification of the Charter, didn't know that future Presidents would send our troops into the no-win Korean and Vietnam wars under UN flags and UN oversight. But, if the warning he issued on July 27, 1945 had been listened to, American forces would never have bled and died in those conflicts. He stated:

> It is also held by some Members of Congress that the United States delegate to the [UN's] Executive Council, in ordering out troops, will act independently of the Congress and without its authority, but will be solely under the orders of the President. This view is held by some on the ground that the President is a symbol of sovereignty, and so has the right to call the Army into war in foreign countries without consulting Congress. It is said that this has been done many times in history. If that doctrine is accepted, the President can take us into war at any time, and the declaration of war by Congress will be simply rubber-stamping the act of the President. Such a doctrine would indicate that many people believe that the Constitution can be changed by customary violations of its limitation of executive power. This, if adhered to, is dangerous doctrine.
>
> ... The control of the war power, as provided in the Constitution, must remain in the Congress if the United States is going to remain a republic.[9]

Senator William Langer (R-ND) voiced similar opposition to UN membership, focusing at one point on the veto power given to five nations. He stated, "if the Charter had been in effect when the American revolution took place, France and all other countries who came to help us would not have been able to come, and today we would still be a colony under the rule of England." Langer certainly favored the idea of our nation being able to act independently.

Langer spoke of the pledges he made to the voters of his state, one of which was that he "would never vote to send our boys away to be slaughtered" on foreign battlefields. He explained:

> Having so pledged myself, and having been elected to my senatorship upon such pledge, and not having been elected to create an organization to which we would give a promise, either express or implied, that it would have authority to send our boys all over the earth, I cannot support the Charter. I believe it is fraught with danger to the American people, and to American institutions.[10]

Senators Shipstead and Langer knew they were swimming against a strong tide of support for the UN. They were up against a carefully created national attitude holding that any gamble, any diplomatic arrangement, or any entanglement, was worth risking in order to forestall future wars. It was no surprise to them when the Senate voted 89-2 to approve the Charter on July 28, 1945. The names of these two farseeing patriots ought to be inscribed on a suitable memorial and placed somewhere right alongside the Declaration of Independence.

But the favorable vote on the UN Charter was not the final step into the world body. That came five months later in a crucially important congressional vote that has been little reported.

The UN Participation Act

During December 1945, there was another opportunity to thwart the designs of world-government enthusiasts. It came when Congress formally voted to take part in UN activities. Members were asked to vote for or against the "UN Participation Act," the kind of measure Senator Wheeler had hoped would reemphasize the sole right of Congress to approve the "size, general readiness and deployment" of any U.S. forces requested by the UN Security Council.

The Act sought to authorize the President to enter into "special" agreements that must be approved by Congress. But, once such an agreement was approved by the President, he would need no further action from Congress to provide military forces at the request of the UN Security Council.

Right from the start of debate about the Act, it became obvious that no interference with the plan to arm the President with power to commit troops to UN duty would be tolerated. Senators Wheeler and Raymond Willis (R-IN) offered an amendment specifically challenging this unconstitutional grab for power by the executive branch. Their proposal sought to require the President to obtain congressional authorization each time he wanted to make U.S. armed forces available to the UN Security Council.

Senator Connally promptly insisted that the Wheeler-Willis

amendment would "kill" the participation program. On December 5, 1945, the *New York Times* said that the President should be "free for prompt and decisive action in international emergencies once the size, state of readiness and general deployment of U.S. peace forces had been approved by the majority votes of the two houses of Congress." This most powerful of all Establishment mouthpieces wanted the forthcoming single vote on the unamended UN Participation Act to constitute a virtual blank check authorizing any future President to commit troops for UN operations any time he wanted to do so.

The Wheeler-Willis amendment went down to defeat by a 65-9 margin. Ever since, Presidents have felt they have the right to send our troops anywhere the UN wants them — without congressional approval. Those who went to fight in Korea or Vietnam can trace their experience, at least in part, to the defeat of this amendment and the passage of the Act. President Bush's insistence that he could commit troops to the war against Iraq reflects back to this congressional abdication of its exclusive power.*

The *New York Times* had earlier branded as "isolationists" any opponents of unfettered presidential power to commit troops to UN operations. The term is still being used today in attempts to silence any American who believes our nation should stay out of the problems in other lands unless they pose a threat to American lives and property.†

Senator Forest C. Donnell (R-MO) then proposed another amendment seeking to require a two-thirds vote of approval in the Senate before any President could supply the UN with our nation's troops. His measure was also defeated, this time by a vote of 57-14 with 13 Republicans joining Democrat Wheeler in one more failed attempt to put a leash on the President's assump-

---

* The nine senators who supported the Wheeler-Willis measure included seven Republicans: Willis (IN), Brooks (IL), Langer (ND), Shipstead (MN), Moore (OK), Revercomb (WV), and Wherry (NE); and two Democrats: Wheeler (MT) and Chavez (NM).

† The word "isolationist" continues to carry an undeserved sting. Wherever it is used, the substitution of the term "non-interventionist" minimizes the problem.

tion of vast power.

While the Senate was debating the UN Participation Act, Senator J. William Fulbright (D-AR) delivered a speech to a businessmen's group in New York City. In that December 11, 1945 speech, he injected atomic weapons into the equation. (Atomic weaponry had not been discussed during the debate about the UN Charter earlier in the year because no such bomb had yet been employed and very few persons even knew such a weapon existed.)

Claiming that the principle of national sovereignty in the era of the atomic bomb was "obsolete," Fulbright urged the creation of an international body under the aegis of the UN to control armaments, and he insisted that no nation should be allowed to veto its decisions. He stated: "The concept of absolute national sovereignty is utterly inconsistent with the creation of effective international rules of conduct which are enforceable."

An ardent supporter of the UN and a confirmed internationalist throughout his years in office, Fulbright had no real interest in maintaining the independence of our nation. His attitude amounted to a complete repudiation of his solemn oath to stand by the Constitution. Sad to say, he was not alone.

On December 18, 1945, the House approved the UN Participation Act by a margin of 344-15. The Senate gave its final approval the following day, and the President signed it on December 20, 1945. Our leaders had significantly increased our nation's entanglement in the UN's web, and Congress had allowed its sole authority to declare war to be assumed by the executive branch.

Senator Dole's Stand Not Good Enough

How deeply are we entangled? Senator Robert Dole (R-KS), the current majority leader of the U.S. Senate, authored an op-ed column for the *New York Times* on January 24, 1994. Based on some of what he stated in that article, one would get the impression that this powerful Senate leader is a strong opponent of our involvement in the UN. But Dole, like so many others, frequently talks a good game but comes up short when meaningful actions are needed. Even what he wrote comes up short of what is needed:

> In the wake of Congressional uproar over American involvement in Somalia, Bosnia and Haiti, some members of Congress are calling for a review of the war powers relationship between Congress and the President. That is fine, but as the blue helmet of the United Nations peacekeepers — heavily subsidized by American greenbacks — turns up in more and more places around the world, it is far more imperative that we redefine the relationship between the United States and the United Nations, and establish a Congressional role in that relationship. As it stands now, the vote of our unelected representative to the UN has the power to commit billions of taxpayer dollars and to risk U.S. soldiers' lives without any say from Congress.[11]

In this column, Dole urges merely that we "redefine" our relationship with the UN. The Republican leader of the Senate mentions and then sidesteps the matter of presidential assumption of the Constitution's exclusive grant of power to Congress to declare war. The real need is for our nation's relationship with the UN to be severed, not redefined. Also, the executive branch must be sharply reined in in accordance with the Constitution, not given equal standing in several vitally important areas.

This is what Senator Dole and all other senators and representatives must be told by their constituents.

Our nation's current "unelected representative to the UN" is Madeleine Albright, another in a long line of veteran CFR members who have held that post. She could veto any measure calling for U.S. funds or the deployment of U.S. troops. But with CFR member Bill Clinton in the White House, and over 400 CFR members serving in U.S. government posts, it is not likely that she will oppose what the UN, the President, and all of the CFR advisers are doing with our money and our troops.*

Before finishing his article, the senator called for making "Congress a full partner in major decisions" regarding the use of

---

* The *1994 CFR Annual Report* claims that 463 of the 3,136 members of this privately run organization are "U.S. government officials."

American soldiers. Congress is not supposed to be "full partner" when men are sent into war; Congress is supposed to be the sole authority in such a decision.

Instead of dabbling at the edges of presidential usurpation of power and UN control of our nation's policies, Senator Dole and others should act as if the nation's continued existence is at stake — because it is. What is needed is nothing less than withdrawal from the UN.

If the UN Participation Act had been rejected in late 1945, there would likely never have been any deployment of U.S. forces in any UN action. This measure was passed by a majority vote in each House of Congress. Therefore, another majority vote in Congress can undo what was done in 1945 and declare this Act null and void.

Such a move by Congress would cripple the designs of the pro-UN, one-world, anti-American forces that have had their way for so many years. Is it really asking too much of our senators and representatives to stand by their oath? Is it asking too much to have them put an end to sending U.S. forces wherever the UN and the President want them?

Presidential power to commit troops at the UN's behest was fully assumed at the start of the Korean War. But even before the outbreak of hostilities in Korea, the forces of world government within our government took another step away from sovereignty with the creation of the North Atlantic Treaty Organization (NATO). Its effect on national sovereignty and our nation's men at arms has been enormous.

In the next chapter, we investigate how our own military was compromised by NATO, totally abused in Korea, and further damaged in Vietnam through our membership in the South East Asia Treaty Organization (SEATO).

CHAPTER 9

NATO and Korea, SEATO and Vietnam

If the incident is permitted to go by without protest, at least from this body, we would have finally terminated for all time the right of Congress to declare war, which is granted to Congress alone by the Constitution of the United States.

— Senator Robert Taft, June 28, 1950

The horrors of World War II had already steered the American people into an acceptance of U.S. membership in the United Nations. An enormous barrage of propaganda about the absolute need for an international force to end for all time the hardships of war worked its sinister magic very well indeed.

But World War II also brought about the rise of the USSR as a world power. In the immediate post-war years, the Soviets swallowed up the nations of Eastern and Central Europe and launched campaigns spreading subversion and terror worldwide. By 1949, China's vast population fell into the hands of the Red menace. A new threat to mankind's peace and prosperity was now stalking the earth.

As far back as the waning days of World War II, important voices in America began pointing out that pro-communist policymakers were manning sensitive positions in our own government. U.S. Ambassador to China Patrick Hurley resigned his post in 1945 and attempted to show that the loss of China had been planned by disloyal personnel in the State Department and in the Far East. He was not alone in directing attention to the policies of Roosevelt/Truman officials that had aided communists in all parts of the world.[1]

Advocates of world government in the West, and especially in the U.S., had actually helped to create the communist menace and feed it with everything imaginable to keep it alive. They then seized upon fear of communist terror as a means of inducing the American people to allow U.S. sovereignty to be compromised and the nation itself to be propelled toward their megalomaniacal goal. As part of this diabolical plan, they created the military alliance known as the North Atlantic Treaty Organization (NATO). Proposed in 1949, it met with only token resistance in Congress.

NATO has always been a creature of the United Nations. Formed under the UN Charter's Chapter VIII (headlined "Regional Arrangements"), NATO is required to adhere to Article 54 of the Charter: "The Security Council shall at all times be kept fully informed of activities undertaken or in contemplation under regional arrangements or by regional agencies...."

NATO's Article 5 pledges all signers to consider an attack on one to be an attack on all. It requires each participating nation to respond militarily to any such incursion. With Soviet troops occupying East Germany, Poland, and other European nations, and even though virtually everything about communism was traceable to the West, these additional threats to Western Europe were real. The question was: Were they something Americans should be required to address with their lives and their treasure?

On July 12, 1949, Senator Robert Taft (R-OH) expressed the view that the creation of NATO amounted to a provocation directed at the USSR. He believed its requirement that the U.S. arm other nations would more likely induce rather than prevent Soviet military action in the region. He proposed adding a reservation to the treaty stipulating that, by signing it, the U.S. would not be committed "morally or legally" to supply arms to NATO's member nations. He was concerned that our arming of nations at or near the USSR's borders would provoke the Soviet leaders to attack our nation as its primary antagonist.

Support for his view came from Senator Kenneth Wherry (R-NE), who asked the Senate: "I should like a very frank reply. What does Article 3 [of the treaty] mean if it does not mean arms?

There should be no evasion of definition. Is this a vehicle for arms, or isn't it?" Taft himself questioned his colleagues, "If there is no such commitment, why not adopt this reservation so there can be no fooling of foreign nations, no misunderstanding anywhere?"

The two senators got little in response except for a reply from prominent internationalist John Foster Dulles, who had been appointed to fill a Senate vacancy by his ideological bedfellow, New York governor Thomas Dewey. Always working for any measure that would steer our nation away from independence and into world government, Dulles described the Taft proposal as "disastrously dangerous." He, of course, should have been expected to hold such a view; he had been present at the 1919 Paris gathering when Edward Mandell House and others decided to form the Council on Foreign Relations; and he was a CFR founding member.

Dulles had earlier told the Senate Foreign Relations Committee that NATO should be operated "not as a military instrument but as a step in a political evolution." He knew, even if many of his colleagues had no such awareness, that the treaty also included a commitment for "economic cooperation," making it a clear path to regional and, eventually, to world government.

Taft argued that other means could be employed to block potential Soviet expansion beyond obligating our nation to collective security. He again warned that NATO "obligates us to go to war if at any time during the next 20 years anyone makes an armed attack on any one of 12 nations." Insisting that sending our men into war is legitimate only "to protect the liberty of our people," he took the occasion afforded during the debate about NATO to criticize the Truman Administration because its leaders

> ... had adopted a tendency to interfere in the affairs of other nations, to assume that we are a kind of demigod and Santa Claus to solve the problems of the world, and that attitude is more and more likely to involve us in disputes where our liberty is not in fact concerned.

But Taft, Wherry, and other opponents of NATO could gather only 13 votes in the Senate on July 12, 1949, and the NATO alliance, created by formal treaty, gained Senate approval. President Truman, now armed with new authority to involve our nation in military and diplomatic adventures, would later rely on the precedent giving him authority to dispatch troops to NATO as authority to send our troops into Korea in the first of America's undeclared wars.

The Korean "Police Action"

The forces of communist North Korea, armed and trained by the USSR, invaded anti-communist South Korea on June 25, 1950. President Truman used his legitimate powers in sending American troops to help remove approximately 2,000 American citizens from the region. Without congressional authorization in the form of a declaration of war, his action should have ceased right there. Almost immediately, however, he converted the mission into full military participation in the war effort. Here's what happened.

On July 27th, the UN Security Council passed a resolution calling on "all members of the UN" to aid South Korea. Summoning congressional leaders to the White House, Mr. Truman outlined his intention to send U.S. forces to South Korea in response to the UN resolution. When House Speaker John McCormack relayed the President's message to the full House, the members stood and cheered. The U.S. Constitution was effectively shoved into a bottom drawer.

The entire nation, much of Congress included, had become terrified by the threat of communism. Yes, the USSR had overrun all of Eastern and Central Europe. Yes, communist forces had recently overrun China and were threatening other nations. Yes, the press was full of factual reports about communist and procommunist traitors operating within our own government.

But the American people hadn't been informed that our own leaders were secretly doing everything they could to keep communism alive and build it into a threatening world power. All through our nation, the people wanted to see something — anything! — done to stop communist progress. Yet, because the U.S.

Constitution was still considered the supreme law of the land by a few legislators, some senators began asking the right questions.

On July 27, 1950, Senator James Kem (R-MO) rose on the floor of the Senate to ask whether the President "has arrogated to himself the authority of declaring war." Springing to Truman's defense, Senator Scott Lucas (D-IL) replied that previous Presidents had frequently used Commander-in-Chief powers to deploy forces without any congressional declaration of war. Senator H. Alexander Smith (R-NJ) agreed with Lucas and actually insisted that the Truman action was in line with U.S. "responsibilities" under the UN Charter. He obviously placed higher value on the UN Charter than he did on the Constitution he had sworn to uphold.

Senator Leverett Saltonstall (R-MA) expressed delight that Mr. Truman had seized "an opportunity to protect the security of the United States and the peace of the world without declaring war or without any desire to go to war." But Senator George Malone (R-NV) immediately saw fit to ask which areas of the earth "were not vital to the security interests of the United States." His concern received support from Senator Eugene Milliken (R-CO), who forthrightly declared that the United States "had no obligation to go to war" in response to North Korea's invasion.

On July 28th, Taft told his colleagues that he would support a declaration of war if one were requested but, referring to the Truman moves, he added that "there is no legal authority for what he has done.... His action unquestionably has brought about a *de facto* war with the government of northern Korea. He has brought that war about without consulting Congress and without congressional approval."[2]

With great foresight, Taft argued: "If the President can intervene in Korea without Congressional approval, he can go to war in Malaya or Indonesia, or Iran or South America."[3] He termed the way the troops were being sent into combat in Korea

> ... a complete usurpation by the President of authority to use the Armed Forces of this country. If the incident is permitted to go by without protest, at least from this body, we would have finally ter-

minated for all time the right of Congress to declare war, which is granted to Congress alone by the Constitution of the United States.[4]

Anyone who wonders under what authority troops were sent to Vietnam, Iraq, Panama, Somalia, Haiti, Bosnia, and elsewhere has the answer. Relying on our nation's presence in the UN and our commitments to the UN regional arrangement NATO, President Truman assumed vast powers *and Congress allowed him to do so*. Congress is still allowing the Constitution to be ignored by Presidents who have seized imperial power and are putting the U.S. military at the disposal of the United Nations.

It is extremely important to realize that of the 50 UN member nations in 1950, the U.S. alone responded initially to the UN's call for troops. (Several nations sent troops later.) Mr. Truman could have declined to provide forces. But, surrounded as he was by CFR members such as Secretary of State Dean Acheson and Assistant Secretary of State for Far Eastern Affairs Dean Rusk, he plunged our nation into the war and trashed the Constitution in the process. The men who were sent to fight paid a heavy price, and so did national sovereignty.

On July 29th, Acheson announced, "All actions taken by the United States to restore the peace in Korea have been under the aegis of the United Nations." He added that it was the policy of our government "to do its utmost to uphold the sanctity of the Charter of the United Nations...."[5]

Also on July 29, 1950, President Truman was asked at a press conference whether our nation was at war. Relying on a phrase first employed by John Foster Dulles in 1945, he answered, "We are not at war; this is a police action."* In response to a further

---

* In his testimony during the 1945 Senate hearings on the UN Charter, Dulles conceded that a major war would require a congressional declaration, but that forces committed to the UN under Article 43 would generally fight "small police actions." See Michael J. Glennon and Allison R. Hayward, "Collective Security and the Constitution," *Georgetown Law Journal*, April 1994, p. 1580. The Dulles-initiated phrase became useful once again when, on September 11, 1994, U.S. Ambassador to the UN Madeleine Albright (CFR) stated on the television program *This Week With David Brinkley* that the impending possible invasion of Haiti would not be a war but "a police action."

inquiry about what authority he was relying on to send troops to Korea, the President said that if he could send troops to NATO, which he had done, he could send troops to Korea.

Senator Taft knew that something was mighty fishy about this entire Korean venture. Over the past few years, our leaders had not only refused to send forces to help Chiang Kai-Shek fight the Chinese Communists, they had refused to provide arms, even those that had been paid for. Taft asked a question that no one answered: "If the United States was not prepared to use its troops and give military assistance to Nationalist China against Chinese Communists, why should it use its troops to defend Nationalist Korea against Korean Communists?"[6]

The Ohio Senator had earlier answered his own question during a 1946 speech given at Kenyon College. Blasting away at the Truman Administration's steady conversion of our nation into the "world's policemen," he thundered:

> This whole policy is no accident. For years we have been accepting at home the theory that the people are too dumb to understand and that a benevolent Executive must be given power to describe policy and administer policy.... Such a policy in the world, as at home, can only lead to tyranny or to anarchy.[7]

Troops Betrayed in "No-Win" War

On July 7, 1950, as American troops were streaming into besieged South Korea, the UN Security Council authorized President Truman to name the commander of UN forces on the scene. Applause was heard in all parts of the nation when the President gave the assignment to General Douglas MacArthur. And even MacArthur was so caught up with anti-communist and pro-UN fervor that he immediately requested 400 UN flags to be sent to Korea so they could be flown by the units in his command.

MacArthur's attitude about the UN was soon to change dramatically. He and his men began to realize that they had been sent to fight and die but were not being permitted to win. Yet, despite increasingly severe restrictions, they did succeed in liberating all of South Korea, and even all of North Korea. By November, North Korea had been defeated and the war had been won. But as one critic later stated, "At that point, we snatched defeat from the jaws of victory." Chinese communist forces poured across the northern border and the war resumed in earnest.

When he was refused permission to destroy the bridges over the Yalu River and denied the help of Chinese Nationalist forces, MacArthur began to express disagreement with the way the war was being directed by Washington. "I realized for the first time," he stated later, "that I had actually been denied the use of my full military power to safeguard the lives of my soldiers and the safety of my army." His dissent, part of which took the form of an appropriate response to House Speaker Joseph Martin's (R-MA) legitimate inquiry, gave President Truman an excuse to remove him from command.

Popular wisdom holds that MacArthur was removed from command on April 11, 1951 for disobeying orders. He never disobeyed; he was such a complete military man that he did not have it in him to do so. He was removed for two reasons: 1) he was making Truman look bad; and 2) he might still have won the war. It is revealing to know that most who believe that MacArthur had no right to disobey and was justly removed are among the most intense proponents of the view that German generals who did obey their civilian commanders during World War II should have disobeyed and were deserving of punishment.

General Matthew Ridgway, soon to be welcomed to CFR membership, was given the UN command. He immediately altered the method of fighting and, in effect, perverted the noble military profession. In his own book, *The Korean War*, Ridgway stated that his first task upon assuming MacArthur's command was "to place reasonable restrictions on the Eighth [U.S. Army] and Republic of Korea Armies' advance." Then he drafted detailed orders to his field commanders telling them, "You will direct the efforts of your forces toward inflicting maximum personnel casualties and material losses on hostile forces in Korea.... Acquisition of terrain in itself is of little or no value."[8]

Classical military strategy includes seizing and holding terrain while destroying both the adversary's capacity and will to fight. But the change Ridgway had mandated reversed that sound strategy. Henceforth, our men were told that killing was their only goal. Eventually they were required to seize positions at great cost, only to abandon what they had seized with no explanation. Most of the casualties in Korea occurred while this indefensible policy was in place.

A morally sound military principle holds that removing an enemy's capability to impose his will should be the goal — *and killing him isn't always necessary*. Making blind killers of men at arms is the ultimate degradation of the military profession.

It was later learned that a Soviet UN official, General Yuri Vasilev, had left his post at UN headquarters in New York in January 1950 and moved to North Korea, where he directed the military buildup of the communist forces. A U.S. Department of Defense release of May 15, 1954 even claimed that Vasilev had given the order in 1950 for the North Koreans to invade. During the war, all military directives sent from Washington and the Pentagon to military commanders in Korea were also supplied to several offices at the UN, including the Military Staff Committee, formerly led by Vasilev and then led by another Soviet General, Ivan Skliaro. Everything the U.S. commanders were doing was known to communist leaders even before actions were taken.

It was also later learned that Chinese General Lin Piao, the commander of the Chinese troops that poured across the Yalu River bridges from Manchuria and slaughtered so many Americans, was able to state in a leaflet distributed in China:

> I would never have made the attack and risked my men and military reputation if I had not been assured that Washington would restrain General MacArthur from taking adequate retaliatory measures against my lines of supply and communication.[9]

After hostilities had ended and more than 50,000 Americans had paid the ultimate price, the generals who had been asked to fight were brought before Congress to tell what had happened. General Mark Clark stated: "I was not allowed to bomb the numerous bridges across the Yalu River over which the enemy constantly poured his trucks, and his munitions, and his killers." General James Van Fleet said: "My own conviction is that there must have been information to the enemy from high diplomatic authorities that we would not attack his home bases across the Yalu."[10]

General Clark amplified Van Fleet's suspicions when he was given the task of negotiating with the North Koreans as the war wound down. He wrote:

> ... perhaps Communists had wormed their way so deeply into our government on both the working and planning levels that they were able to exercise an inordinate degree of power in shaping the course of America ... I could not help wondering and worrying whether we were faced with open enemies across the conference table and hidden enemies who sat with us in our most secret councils.[11]

Air Force General George Stratemeyer added: "You get in war to win it. You do not get in war to stand still and lose it, and we were required to lose it." And General MacArthur summarized: "Such a limitation upon the utilization of available military force to repel an enemy attack has no precedent, either in our own history, or, so far as I know, in the history of the world."[12]

MacArthur was correct about there being no precedent for limiting the use of available forces in war. What he did not know was that the precedents established in Korea would be repeated in another no-win war in Vietnam. One Korean War precedent involved giving the Chinese communists a safe sanctuary across the Yalu River in Manchuria from which they mounted their attack on our forces, built up their supplies, and planned their moves. Orders keeping our forces out of the enemy's territory would be repeated in Vietnam. And victory was never the goal.

The fighting in Korea ended in 1953. But there has been no peace treaty, and the state of war still exists in a technical sense.

It is also important to realize that all military personnel serving in Korea from 1950 onward have served in the "United Nations Command," not in any United States command. For more than 40 years, troops sent to Korea have been transferred to UN jurisdiction without any being asked if they had any objection.

Our nation's experiences in the Korean War should have completely destroyed any credibility possessed by the United Nations. But, beginning in 1953, U.S. leaders included President Dwight Eisenhower and Secretary of State John Foster Dulles, both of whom were members of the CFR. Their commitment to the goals of the CFR included unquestioning support for and defense of the United Nations. And under their leadership, the Southeast Asia Treaty Organization (SEATO) was created in 1954. It was under SEATO that the next no-win war was launched in Vietnam.

Looking back with the benefit of years of hindsight, it seems clear that the United Nations wasn't using our troops for its purposes during the Korean conflict. The UN was still finding its way toward legitimacy and acceptance by many nations after only five years of existence. The deeper treachery was that partisans for world government within our nation's leadership used the opportunity afforded by the United Nations to compromise the U.S. Constitution, chip away at national sovereignty, and establish precedents for further transfer of our military to the world body.

In effect, the UN didn't govern U.S. policy regarding our participation in the Korean War. Our own leaders controlled it — and they could hardly have done a worse job for the nation and especially for the troops who did the fighting. But their failures weren't caused by ineptitude; a hidden agenda guided every action taken. The American people believed that our leaders would do everything possible to win the war against communism, protect the well-being of our troops, adhere to their oath to the Constitution, and protect the sovereignty of this nation. In every case, the people were betrayed. And the betrayals accomplished during the Korean War were repeated and magnified in succeeding years.

No-Win War #2: Vietnam

By the late 1950s, much of the bitterness stemming from the mishandling of the Korean War had faded. But the threat of communism was still dominating America's thinking. Cuba's fall to Castro in 1959 and Castro's eventual admission that he had been a communist all his adult life increased fear of communist might. But most Americans were not aware that Castro's rise to power had been accomplished with pivotal assistance from the U.S. State Department, whose key personnel had certain evidence that he was a communist.*

In the Far East, U.S. forces had for years been involved in steadily escalating military activity in South Vietnam. Yet, it was not until Congress was stampeded into passing the Tonkin Gulf Resolution on August 7, 1964 that the enormous buildup of men and material began. Though this much-heralded resolution was touted as a declaration of war, it was nothing of the kind. What it really amounted to was a congressional green light for the civilian leaders of the military to intensify the war, silence principled opposition, lead the nation closer to world government, and replace real military professionals with politicians in uniform who were willing to have our nation's armed forces improperly used once again.

The Tonkin Gulf Resolution was very much the same as the ill-fated congressional acquiescence given to President Truman's "police action" in Korea. The measure was steamrolled through Congress in the wake of an attack on U.S. destroyers that never actually occurred. Admiral James Stockdale was a Navy pilot on the scene during the alleged assault. After returning from seven

---

* Former U.S. Ambassador to Cuba Earl E.T. Smith told of his early warnings to Washington about Castro's commitment to communism *before* the bearded dictator took control. Despite warnings from Smith and others including John Birch Society founder Robert Welch, the State Department — led by CFR founder and devoted member John Foster Dulles and aided by CIA Director Allen Dulles, his equally committed CFR member brother — successfully arranged for Castro to seize Cuba. See Earl E.T. Smith, *The Fourth Floor*, 1962, Random House, New York, NY; Robert Welch, "We Pause To Remark," *American Opinion* magazine, September 1958.

years as a POW in North Vietnam, he reported in his own book that he was actually flying a patrol mission over the scene at the time. He insisted that there were no North Vietnamese vessels in the area and, therefore, none were firing at our ships.[13]

Numerous statements from Johnson Administration officials relied totally on our commitment to SEATO and its UN parent for authority to proceed with the war. The State Department's Bulletin #8062, issued on March 28, 1966, stated: "The Southeast Asia Collective Defense treaty authorizes the President's actions. The Southeast Asia Treaty Organization was designed as a collective defense arrangement under Article 51 of the UN Charter.... The United States has reported to the Security Council on measures it has taken in countering Communist aggression in Vietnam."

Mr. Johnson himself proclaimed on January 10, 1967, "We are in Vietnam because the United States and our allies are committed by the SEATO treaty to act to meet the common danger of aggression in Southeast Asia."

There were no UN flags flying this time, and hardly anyone in America knew that our leaders were relying on the UN for authority to be involved. But the restrictions on the men in the front lines were even more severe than those faced a decade earlier in Korea. Generals who protested were cashiered, the most prominent being Marine Corps General Lewis Walt, who was in line to become the Marine Corps Commandant, but who was passed over for a man more willing to abide by the changing rules. Once again, the enemy was afforded privileged sanctuaries in Laos and in the demilitarized zone (DMZ). Our men were not permitted to attack enemy strongholds and, essentially, had to fight with one hand tied behind their backs.

Keith William Nolan vividly tells what it was like to serve in Vietnam in his book, *Operation Buffalo*. He quotes Marine Corporal J. Larry Stuckey's recollections:

> Being a Navy Cross winner, a lot of people expect me to say I'd do it all again. I wish I could, but I can't. The thought from Operation

> Buffalo of a field, about half the size of a football field, littered with dead Marines from Bravo Company, will not permit me to say I'd do it all again. I can never forget stacking their bodies three and four deep on top of a tank to get them out and home. My willingness to swear blind, undying allegiance to this country's foreign policies died in Vietnam. I have not deserted my country, but rather my country deserted me when I needed it the most. This government allowed thousands of men to place their lives on the line in a war in which the government knew there was never a strategic plan to win. Surely our leaders would not let us die for nothing. But they did.[14]

Corporal Stuckey errs. Those Marines did not die "for nothing." They died to advance the sinister plan to build the new world order. The problem is that neither they nor Corporal Stuckey knew such a plan existed.

Nolan's book also contains the following passage describing the difficult task of keeping troop morale high:

> One day, with the same purpose in mind, Gen. William Childs Westmoreland helicoptered into lonely, little Con Thien. Major Danielson escorted Westmoreland around the perimeter. When a Marine pointedly asked, "General, I lost my best buddy to incoming [artillery fire] yesterday — why can't we go into the DMZ after those b******s?" Danielson said, "The general's response was, 'Son, I wish we could, but the politics of the situation are such that we can't violate the DMZ.' Can you imagine how frustrating that response was to a young, dirty, unshaven, bleary-eyed, thirsty Marine?"

In 1985, Senator Barry Goldwater (R-AZ) pried the Vietnam War's official "Rules of Engagement" out of the State Department. Published in the *Congressional Record*, they show that our own leaders made defeat for the U.S. forces and victory for the communist North Vietnamese inevitable.[15] The UN was not mentioned in connection with these incredible rules because they were the creation of our own officials led by Secretary of State Dean Rusk and Secretary of Defense Robert McNamara, and accepted by Generals Lyman Lemnitzer, Maxwell Taylor, William Westmoreland, and Andrew Goodpaster — all of whom were CFR members.

U.S. pilots were forbidden to bomb Soviet-made SAM missile sites under construction, but they could risk their lives flying into launched missiles after the sites became operational. They were not allowed to destroy communist aircraft on the ground but were permitted to attack any that were armed and in the air. Truck depots 200 yards away from a main road were forbidden targets; trucks on the road could be attacked. Pilots flying over supply ships on their way to North Vietnam's Haiphong harbor were not permitted to attack even though they knew these vessels were laden with war materials sent by Eastern European communist nations for use against Americans.

Throughout the war, returning troops told of being ordered not to shoot until shot at, not to attack the enemy's privileged sanctuaries, and not to hold terrain that had been won at great cost in lives and effort. Just as General Ridgway had done with the troops under his command in Korea, orders were given to conduct "search and destroy" missions. Classical military strategy went out the window once again.

While all this was going on, the Johnson Administration increased aid and trade with the Eastern European nations supplying the North Vietnamese. On October 6, 1966, the President himself declared in a speech to the National Conference of Editorial Writers: "We intend to press for legislative authority to negotiate trade agreements which could extend most-favored-nation tariff treatment to European Communist states [and] reduce export controls on East-West trade with respect to hundreds of nonstrategic items."

Six days later, the *New York Times* reported:

> The United States put in effect today one of President Johnson's proposals for stimulating East-West trade by removing restrictions on the export of more than four hundred commodities to the Soviet Union and Eastern Europe....

> Poland and Romania have been given special treatment, and, in general, the result of today's measure will be to extend such treatment to the Soviet Union, Hungary, Bulgaria, Czechoslovakia, Albania, and Mongolia.

During war, there are no "non-strategic items." Trade with these nations, the undeniable source of North Vietnam's war machine, led to the deaths of many Americans. But, with Department of Commerce clearance, American firms boosted shipments to the communist regimes in Europe of such items as ball bearings, rocket engines, radar devices, computers, steel and aluminum tubing, machine tools, etc. On October 13, 1966, Congressman John Ashbrook (R-OH) focused on just one item in his angry message to fellow congressmen:

> The machine tool industry can rejuvenate itself, for machine tools can build machine tools. Machine tools are needed to build guns, tanks, and missiles.... In short the machine tool is the principal sinew of war. One expert declared before a Senate subcommittee some years ago that he would rather send them a missile than a machine tool, because a missile is fired and expended but machine tools will produce a rifle or a missile over and over again.

President Johnson's efforts to increase trade with the communist nations in Europe had a profound effect. And they were not totally unknown. On December 26, 1966, the *Chicago Tribune* reported:

> Weapons of the Polish armed forces are being shipped from Stettin harbor in Poland in ever increasing quantities to North Vietnam harbors.... While on one side of the Stettin harbor American wheat is being unloaded from freighters, on the other side of the same harbor weapons are loaded which are being used against American soldiers.

By February 15, 1967, driven by frustration over his inability to have the Administration's policies changed, Congressman H.R.

Gross (R-IA) dared tell fellow congressmen what few would even consider:

> It is time that the citizens of this country were made to understand that they and their fighting men have been made the victims of a betrayal to international politics and intrigue.[16]

"Betrayal" may be a strong word but, in this instance, it was the correct word.

Members of The John Birch Society collected millions of signatures on a petition to Congress to stop aid and trade with communist nations. When it began to have a beneficial effect, the State Department issued a pamphlet entitled *Private Boycotts Versus the Public Interest* which denounced Americans who criticized policies that were contributing to the death of our forces in Vietnam. And, in November 1966, U.S. Ambassador to the USSR Averell Harriman (CFR) told the nation via television that opponents of trading with communists were "bigoted, pig-headed people who don't know what's going on in the world...."[17]

While good men were dying at the hands of communist forces equipped with weaponry traceable to U.S. aid and trade, military leaders of the old-style began to speak out. Journalist Lloyd Mallan interviewed many high-ranking officers and reported their attitudes about the war in an explosive article published in the March 1968 *Science & Mechanics* magazine. He summarized the conclusions of these military professionals:

> The war against Vietnam can be irrevocably won in six weeks ... the remaining Vietcong guerrillas in the South could be conquered within six months ... [the war] may go on for another five, ten or more years — if it continues to be fought as at present.... We are fighting a war in a weak-sister manner that is unprecedented throughout the history of military science.

Mallan stressed that he had spoken individually with these "most experienced and astute military strategists," and that none knew what the others had stated. He then named the men who had reached the above conclusion. They included former Joint Chiefs of Staff Chairman General Nathan Twining, former Chief of Naval Operations Admiral Arleigh Burke, former Army Chief of Staff General George H. Decker, former Air Force Vice Chief of Staff Frederick H. Smith, former Commander in Chief of the Strategic Air Force General Thomas S. Power, former Army Chief of Research and Development Lieutenant General Arthur G. Trudeau, and several others whose names were not revealed because they were still on active duty and feared reprisals.

How could victory have been achieved? Former Air Force Chief of Staff General Curtis LeMay's plan was published in the October 10, 1966 *U.S. News & World Report*. Declaring that he had lost patience with the Administration's "half measures" that were costing lives and wasting money, he said we should hit the enemy hard, "destroy his economy and his will to wage war." He wrote:

> Suppose, for example, that we should progressively bomb command and control centers, airfields, electrical-power installations, factories, major supply-storage areas, irrigation systems, principal transportation centers, and the harbor facilities at Haiphong.
>
> Could Hanoi continue to reinforce and supply an army of 90,000 in the South? Could she even feed her civilian population? Can there be any question but that either the Ho Chi Minh Government would sue for peace, or another government would overthrow Ho and accept the conference table alternative?

What LeMay called for wasn't done because the last thing on the minds of the Administration officials was victory.

On July 23, 1966, President Lyndon Johnson was campaigning for Great Society congressmen. In a speech he gave at Fort Campbell, Kentucky, the home of one of the divisions fighting in Vietnam, he paid tribute to the men who were 10,000 miles from home fighting a war, while he told those before him that "our diplomats are probing for a way to make an honorable peace desirable to the communist leaders in Hanoi."

Why not victory? Why should we try to please the enemy? What was this unusual war all about?

The Hidden Goal

There has always been a hidden goal behind helping communists to take control of nations, building the USSR and its satellite empire into a world-class power, and assisting the entire Soviet bloc to make war on America in Vietnam. That goal has been to force the American people to want world government. The directors of our end of this struggle sought to convince Americans that communist military might was virtually invincible.

In March 1962, a U.S. State Department report entitled *A World Effectively Controlled by the United Nations* reached selected government personnel. Funded by taxpayers and authored by CFR member Lincoln P. Bloomfield, it was originally classified and not intended for public consumption. It therefore was written in plain and direct language. While it contains a great deal of extremely revealing attitudes and admissions, Bloomfield supplied the underlying reason why our government was helping communism. He stated: "... if the communist dynamic were greatly abated, the West might lose whatever incentive it has for world government."*

Translated, this meant that our government should help communists to enslave billions of human beings and threaten the rest of the world in order to drive the West, especially the United States, into world government. It meant sending hundreds of thousands of Americans to death and injury in contrived no-win wars in order to solidify the belief that communist power was so great that world government was the only alternative. If this does not supply strong evidence that a conspiracy against the American people was being carried out by their own government, nothing does.

---

* The document's origins are given in its pages as follows: "Prepared for the Institute for Defense Analyses in support of a study submitted to the Department of State under contract No. SCC 28270, dated February 24, 1961."

Finally, the war ended, our forces came home, and South Vietnam, Laos, and Cambodia were swallowed up by communism. Since the world government promoters no longer needed SEATO, it was disbanded.

In April 1969, the number of Americans in Vietnam reached a peak of 543,000. Before the war ended in 1973, the final toll of casualties numbered 58,000 dead and 153,000 wounded. The crime is that we could have won the war. The even greater crime consisted of the lie that world government was necessary.

What happened in Korea and Vietnam was made possible by our nation's entry into the UN, congressional passage of the UN Participation Act of December 1945, the 1949 creation of NATO and the transfer of war-making powers to the President, the congressional acquiescence to President Truman's act of sending our forces into the Korean War (what Truman called a "police action") and the 1954 creation of SEATO with its additional transfers of war-making authority from Congress to the President.

All of this was ultimately the work of the world government promoters who could be found swarming all over our nation's capital. It was they who arranged our undeclared wars. Whenever any U.S. troops are called on to fight, they should be backed up by a congressional declaration of war which would, by definition, contain a commitment to win — and win swiftly. But this is not the way things were done in Korea or Vietnam.

As stated earlier, winning in either Korea or Vietnam was never the goal. Instead, the forces denying victory sought to reap the many benefits they could derive from involvement in no-win wars. They succeeded in changing the role of our military, altering the type of officers placed in command of the military, even changing the reason for the existence of the armed services. And, as Robert Taft had declared in 1950, a huge overall step toward world government came when Congress abandoned its responsibility and permitted presidential action that "terminated for all time the right of Congress to declare war, which is granted to Congress alone by the Constitution of the United States."

Was Taft's statement accurate? Has the congressional power to declare war been "terminated for all time"? Will Congress continue to allow the placement of our nation's military at the service of the United Nations?

Or, did the Ohio senator overstate the case? Are there not enough real Americans still left in this country to force Congress and the President to abide by the limitations in the Constitution? Let us hope so. And let us find these real Americans and activate them in programs to change the direction of our nation.

In today's world, a nation without control of its own military arm will not be a nation for very long. Rapidly unfolding events and an array of dangerous precedents now have the American people facing the very real prospect of seeing UN troops from other nations enforcing UN edicts within the borders of the United States. And our own sons might soon be ordered to perform similar missions for the UN in other lands. Obviously, there are no alternatives but to reinstate the Constitution's proper restraints over the use of this nation's armed forces and to make it known that uninvited foreign troops will never be allowed within our borders.

While the horrendous misuse of our military forces was being accomplished, while Congress was ceding its authority to the President and the United Nations, and while good men were being sent into a no-win meat grinder in Southeast Asia, a progression of Presidents and Administration officials began implementing a plan to turn our forces formally and completely over to UN control.

We examine the little-known, incredibly important, and highly treasonous 1961 *U.S. Program for General and Complete Disarmament in a Peaceful World* in the next chapter.

Chapter 10

Disarmament for All Except the UN

The program to be presented to this Assembly for general and complete disarmament under effective international control ... would achieve, under the eyes of an international disarmament organization, a steady reduction in force, both nuclear and conventional, until it has abolished all armies and all weapons except those needed for internal order and a new United Nations Peace Force.

— President John F. Kennedy
Address to the UN General Assembly
September 25, 1961

President Kennedy formally presented the U.S. disarmament program to the United Nations immediately after delivering the speech cited above. Authored by the State Department, its title is *Freedom From War: The United States Program for General and Complete Disarmament In a Peaceful World*. It also carries the designation *Department of State Publication 7277*. (The full text of this sovereignty-destroying document is reprinted in Appendix B.)

As the President stated, the program's goal is "a steady reduction in force" leading to a condition where the entire world "has abolished all weapons except those needed for internal order and a new United Nations Peace Force."

It all sounds so idealistic. But wait a minute! Isn't this program misnamed? As President Kennedy indicated, it calls for complete disarmament but it makes an exception for weapons "needed for internal order and a new United Nations Peace Force."

This is not a program for "general and complete disarmament; it is a program for *selective* disarmament. It is not about weapons elimination; it is about weapons distribution. And it does not propose scrapping all weapons; it proposes scrapping all but those retained for internal order and the United Nations.

Further, it is clear that the disarmament features of this program are to apply only to nations, not to the world body. The United States is certainly one of those nations. If carried out as written, the program would ensure that the United Nations alone possesses military might. That would give the UN the capability of ruling the world.

This is what John Kennedy proposed. And, as unbelievable as it may seem, this is the program our leaders have been implementing for the past three decades. Top officials of the U.S. government really intend to disarm our country and make the UN the world's unchallengeable ruler. They must be stopped before our nation is fully disarmed, and before blue-helmeted UN troops arrive to seize control of our nation for the world government plotters who are behind this treasonous scheme.

"Fixed and Determined" Policy

A few months after the unveiling of this treasonous program, Senator Joseph Clark (D-PA) referred to it in a speech to the Senate. On March 1, 1962, he approvingly reminded his colleagues that this program is "the fixed and determined policy of the government of the United States." Unfortunately, Clark was correct.

The program was then rewritten in greater detail and renamed *Blueprint for the Peace Race: Outline of Basic Provisions of a Treaty on General and Complete Disarmament in a Peaceful World* and presented by President Kennedy to an 18-nation disarmament conference held in Geneva, Switzerland on April 18, 1962. The *Blueprint* did not cancel any portion of its predecessor. As stated in its Foreword, it merely "elaborates and extends the proposals of September 25, 1961."

When questioned about this program, Arms Control and Disarmament Agency General Council A. Richard Richstein confirmed in a May 11, 1982 letter that "the United States has never formally withdrawn this proposal."[1]

Additional testimony about the continued existence of this program has been supplied by the chief historian of the Arms Control and Disarmament Agency, Dr. William Nary. "The program has not been withdrawn and some of its steps have been implemented," stated Dr. Nary in a telephone conversation with this author on November 1, 1993.

It obviously behooves any American to examine this suicidal program in detail so that it can be combated intelligently.

Incredible Objectives

The *Freedom From War* program lists four overall "objectives," the first of which reads:

> *(a) The disbanding of all national armed forces and the prohibition of their reestablishment in any form whatsoever other than those required to preserve internal order and for contributions to a United Nations Peace Force;*

This means no more U.S. Army, Navy, Air Force or Marine Corps controlled by this nation. The only "national armed forces" permitted would be 1) those comprising a national police force "to preserve internal order," and 2) those supplied as "contributions" to the UN for its Peace Force.

What this also means is that a cardinal feature of a totalitarian state will be created. According to this program, preserving internal order will become the responsibility of the "national armed forces" permitted to remain in existence. This remnant will, therefore, constitute a national police force assigned to preserve "internal order."

In Hitler's Germany, this function was carried out by the Gestapo; in Soviet Russia, it was accomplished by the KGB; and in Communist China, all police power for maintaining internal order is also controlled nationally. Police power in nations where the people are free is always locally controlled, as it has always been in the United States.

Other than those forces permitted to exist in a national police force, the American military units not disbanded will be contributed to the UN for its Peace Force. Personnel in these units will be American citizens, but they will be required to do the will of the United Nations.

Another of the "objectives" of this incredible program reads:

> *(b) The elimination from national arsenals of all armaments, including all weapons of mass destruction and the means for their delivery, other than those required for a United Nations Peace Force and for maintaining internal order;*

Not only will nations be required to disband whatever armed forces they have created to defend themselves, they must divest themselves of all armaments earmarked for national defense. The UN will take no chances that weapons sitting around in some arsenal, especially weapons of "mass destruction," might fall into the hands of anyone who would use them to oppose the UN.

The presumption here, of course, is that the people will naïvely believe that weapons are used only to commit acts of aggression. But weapons also serve the very important purpose of preventing aggression. In other words, weapons are needed for self-defense. The United Nations, however, is to be all-powerful and no one is to have the capability to defend his nation, himself, or his family from its designs.

The next of these "objectives" addresses the need for "compliance" with UN-imposed obligations. It mandates:

> *(c) The establishment and effective operation of an International Disarmament Organization within the framework of the United Nations to ensure compliance at all times with all disarmament obligations;*

The UN does not intend to take any chances. Therefore, this program calls for an "international" snooping agency empowered to "ensure compliance" with each of the above "obligations."

No formal group known as the "International Disarmament Organization" has been formed, but several existing UN creations have the potential of becoming exactly what this portion of the overall plan calls for. These are the International Atomic Energy Agency, the UN Disarmament Commission, and the peacekeeping functions of the Military Staff Committee.

Whatever this supranational agency is called, it will, of necessity, operate with powers that supersede the laws and prerogatives of any government — certainly including the government of this nation.

From May 23 to July 1, 1978, the UN convened its first-ever Special Session of the General Assembly on Disarmament at UN headquarters in New York. Delegates agreed to a 129-paragraph "Final Document" whose Paragraph No. 111 reads almost exactly like the final goals of the Kennedy disarmament program. This portion of the document states:

> General and complete disarmament under strict and effective international control shall permit States to have at their disposal only those non-nuclear forces, armaments, facilities and establishments as are agreed to be necessary to maintain internal order and protect the personal security of citizens and in order that States shall support and provide agreed manpower for a United Nations peace force.

In recent years, the UN Disarmament Commission has begun to target private ownership of arms as a response to "illicit arms trade." A March 22, 1994 "working paper" written by the delegate to the UN from Colombia that addressed this topic was immediately circulated by the Commission. It holds that the "State should exercise absolute control over the manufacture of arms, the arms trade, and the possession and use of arms." All of this, of course, is a response to "illicit trafficking." But it leads to disarming private citizens.[2]

And, finally, the fourth of the 1961 disarmament plan's "objectives" reads:

(d) The institution of effective means for the enforcement of international agreements, for the settlement of disputes, and for the maintenance of peace in accordance with the principles of the United Nations.

The UN delights in using the word "enforcement." So, that's the term chosen by the authors of this U.S. plan. The UN intends to have peace enforced by a UN Peace Force made up of individuals from the various nations whose services have been given as "contributions" to the world body.

The peace being sought will always be in accord with the principles of the United Nations. As to what those principles might include, a quick look at Chapter VII of the UN Charter reveals that the "peace" organization retains for itself the power to determine what might constitute 1) any threat to peace, 2) any breach of peace, or 3) any act of aggression.

Once having decided that its definition of peace is not being adhered to, the UN claims authority in Article 42 of the Charter to "take such action by air, sea, or land forces as may be necessary" to restore its idea of peace. That's not peace; that's war.

The "peace" organization is not interested in the kind of peace sought by normal individuals. Its very Charter outlines procedures enabling it to enforce and maintain its unimpeded rule over the planet with military action.

And, we are sad to report, this entire program is the "fixed and determined policy" of the government of the United States. It is the intention of our leaders to implement every portion of the objectives we have just presented.

Specifics Spelled Out

Toward the end of this ten-page document, the Kennedy administration's State Department subversives wrote the following:

In Stage III progressive controlled disarmament ... would proceed to a point where no state would have the military power to challenge the progressively strengthened U.N. Peace Force....

Make no mistake about it: No nation — ours certainly included — would be permitted to retain a military capability to defend itself. No force on earth would be permitted to "challenge" the UN Peace Force. *Freedom From War* continues:

> *The manufacture of armaments would be prohibited except for those of agreed types and quantities to be used by the U.N. Peace Force and those required to maintain internal order. All other armaments would be destroyed or converted to peaceful purposes.*

Note that there is no allowance here for private ownership of arms. Under this program, no one will be permitted to defend himself or his property. There will be no God-given and constitutionally protected "right to keep and bear arms." Other than the UN Peace Force, the only possessor of weaponry of any consequence will be the UN-controlled national police force formed to "maintain internal order."

This portion of the world-government disarmament scheme was spelled out far more clearly by Wall Street lawyer Grenville Clark and Professor Louis B. Sohn in their 1958 work entitled *World Peace Through World Law*. Clark was vice president of the UN-promoting World Federalist Association and Sohn a member of the CFR. Their detailed recommendations for disarming individuals and arming the UN included the following statement: "No nation shall allow the possession by any public or private organization or individual of any military equipment whatsoever or of any arms except such small arms as are reasonably needed by duly licensed hunters or by duly licensed individuals for personal protection." Their book even outlines procedures for hauling into UN-run courts any "individuals accused of violating provisions" of regulations set by the UN. Licensing would obviously become a significant tool with which to disarm the people.[3]

Then, the final sentence in this incredible document spells out the ultimate goal:

> *The peace-keeping capabilities of the United Nations would be suf-*

ficiently strong and the obligations of all states under such arrangements sufficiently far-reaching as to assure peace ... in a disarmed world.

Peace, peace, peace! There will be peace all right, the peace of submission, even the peace of the grave.

The *Freedom From War* program lays out the successive steps to be taken on the way to complete disarmament, many of which have already been fashioned into treaties binding our nation. Whether or not other nations signing these treaties have abided by them is a wholly separate matter. The point is that our nation continues to implement the program it fashioned in 1961, the period when the Cold War threat of Soviet military might was at its highest point. It certainly mattered little to the authors and implementers of this plan that our nation might be victimized by communist power or by a communist bluff.

Freedom From War calls for banning nuclear testing, so our nation followed with the Nuclear Test-Ban Treaty. Other steps called for in this document have been addressed by such pacts as the treaty banning the use of outer space for nuclear weapons, the Nuclear Non-Proliferation Treaty, and the Intermediate Nuclear Forces Treaty of 1988. Whatever appears in the 1961 program eventually shows up as part of our nation's policy.

If this program is not derailed soon, Americans will be forced to say good-bye to national sovereignty; good-bye to God-given rights protected by the U.S. Constitution; good-bye to freedoms too often taken for granted; good-bye to the inheritance every American received from our nation's brave and far-seeing founders; and good-bye to any chance to pass that inheritance on to children, grandchildren, and generations yet to come.

Who Concocted This Nightmare?

Official responsibility for this *selective* disarmament program lies with President Kennedy, Secretary of State Dean Rusk, and Secretary of Defense Robert S. McNamara. Each held membership in the Council on Foreign Relations.[4]

The identity of all who participated in the creation of *Freedom From War* has never been publicized. However, it is certain that its primary authors were John J. McCloy and Arthur H. Dean. At the time, McCloy was already serving as the chairman of the board of the CFR, and Dean was a member of the CFR's board.

When President Kennedy assumed office in 1961, he named McCloy as his chief disarmament adviser. As far back as 1944, when serving as an Assistant Secretary of War, McCloy approved an order permitting communists to serve as officers in the U.S. military. In 1945, he participated as a member of the U.S. delegation at the UN's founding conference.

In 1950, McCloy helped to found World Brotherhood, an organization defending the rights of communists while favoring world government. He eventually rose to chairmanship of the board of trustees of both the Ford Foundation and the Atlantic Institute. His authorship of *Freedom From War* is completely consistent with his lifetime of opposition to national independence and support for the world government.

Arthur H. Dean served as vice chairman of the Institute for Pacific Relations during the late 1940s when the organization was described by congressional committees as being substantially under communist control. A member of the United Nations Association of the United States, he too has always strongly favored the world body at the expense of our nation's independence.

Another CFR member who helped with this proposal was Harlan Cleveland, appointed by President Kennedy in February 1961 as Assistant Secretary of State for International Organizations and UN Affairs. When the State Department's own security division refused Cleveland a security clearance because of his known association with subversives, Secretary of State Dean Rusk (CFR) personally waived the clearance requirement. Cleveland then attempted to have the government rehire convicted Soviet spy Alger Hiss.

Harlan Cleveland was responsible for bringing Richard N. Gardner (CFR) into government as the Deputy Assistant Secretary of State for International Organizations. In his 1964 book *In*

Pursuit of World Order (which carried a Foreword by Cleveland), Gardner stated, "Discussion of whether or not we should be in the United Nations is about as useful as discussion of whether or not we should have a U.S. Congress."[5] In his book, Gardner boasted of helping to shape U.S. policy in several areas, including disarmament. In 1974, he spelled out his disdain for the American system when he advocated strengthening the UN and performing "an end run around national sovereignty, eroding it piece by piece."

A Stacked Deck

When the UN was being organized, officials of the Soviet Union, the United States, and the other three permanent Security Council member-states (Great Britain, France, and Nationalist China) agreed that the USSR should have the responsibility of naming the individual who would fill the critically important post of UN Undersecretary for Political and Security Council Affairs. The holder of this post is charged by the UN with overseeing all of its military and police functions. He also wields jurisdiction for the world body in the areas of disarmament and atomic energy.

In his book, *In the Cause of Peace*, Trygve Lie, the UN's first Secretary General, detailed his amazement that the United States would agree to such an arrangement. He wrote:

> Mr. Vyshinsky [of the USSR] did not delay his approach. He was the first to inform me of an understanding which the Big Five had reached in London on the appointment of a Soviet national as assistant secretary-general for political and security council affairs....
>
> Mr. Stettinius confirmed to me that he had agreed with the Soviet delegation in the matter....
>
> The preservation of international peace and security was the organization's highest responsibility, and it was to entrusting the direction of the Secretariat department most concerned with this to a Soviet national that the Americans had agreed.[6]

Starting in 1946, with the full approval of our nation's delegates, the Soviets named one communist after another to hold this strategically important post. In 1992, the responsibilities were divided for the first time with former Soviet Deputy Foreign Minister Vladimir E. Petrovsky sharing the post with James O.C. Jonah of Sierra Leone. Petrovsky will oversee military and disarmament matters in all areas of the world except Africa and Asia, the two regions to be watched over by Jonah.

UN Undersecretary for Political and Security Council Affairs

1946-49 ...... Arkady Sobolev, USSR
1949-53 ...... Konstantin Zinchenko, USSR
1953-54 ...... Ilya Tchernychev, USSR
1954-57 ...... Dragoslav Protitch, Yugoslavia
1957-60 ...... Anatoly Dobrynin, USSR
1960-62 ...... Georgy Arkadev, USSR
1962-63 ...... E.D. Kiselev, USSR
1963-65 ...... V.P. Suslov, USSR
1965-68 ...... Alexei E. Nesterenko, USSR
1968-73 ...... Leonid Kutakov, USSR
1973-78 ...... Arkady N. Shevchenko, USSR
1978-81 ...... Mikhail D. Sytenko, USSR
1981-86 ...... Viacheslav A. Ustinov, USSR
1987-92 ...... Vasily S. Safronchuk, USSR
1992- ...... Vladimir E. Petrovsky, USSR
James O. C. Jonah, Sierra Leone

When our troops went to war in Korea under the UN, the top UN military officer happened to be Konstantin Zinchenko of the Soviet Union, the government that had armed and trained North Korea's troops. Zinchenko certainly favored the North Korean side wherever he could.

The UN Charter requires that every step our forces took in the Korean War had to be reported to the United Nations. The Soviets, therefore, were able to rely on Konstantin Zinchenko to keep them informed of U.S. plans. As we indicated in the previous chapter, General James Van Fleet told a congressional committee after the war, "My own conviction is that there must have been information to the enemy from high diplomatic authorities that we would not attack his home bases across the Yalu River."[7]

The deck was stacked against our troops in Korea. And it was equally stacked against our men in Vietnam, where our SEATO obligation required us to report every planned step to the UN. Soviet nationals Arkadev, Kiselev, Suslov, Nesterenko, and Kutakov were in position to transmit U.S. plans to compatriots in North Vietnam.

Summing Up

- Our leaders have been working for three decades both to disarm this nation and to turn over our armed forces to the United Nations.
- The program to which they are committed will make the United Nations the most powerful entity on earth, able to force its will on us and on the rest of mankind.
- The program also calls for disarming all citizens and creating a centralized police force in each nation subservient to the United Nations.
- Ever since the founding of the UN, its Undersecretary for Political and Security Council Affairs — the post charged with overseeing all military, disarmament and police functions — has by agreement been in the hands of a communist.
- The individuals who concocted this nightmarish scheme are members of the world-government-promoting Council on Foreign Relations.
- All of this supplies evidence of a conspiracy against the independence of our nation and the freedom of the American people.

The way out of this trap begins with alerting many more Americans, changing the leadership of Congress via the ballot box, and withdrawing our nation from the clutches of the United Nations.

Time is running out.

The Council on Foreign Relations has extremely strong influence in government, the media, the academic world, the foundations, and the multinational corporate world. Its determined leaders have also pulled within their net many of the highest ranking and most influential military leaders. In effect, they have politicized the military profession and created support for the goal of world government.

How the military has become dominated by the CFR is the subject of the next chapter.

Chapter 11

Politicizing the Generals and Admirals

[A] careful examination of what is happening behind the scenes reveals that all of these interests are working in concert with the masters of the Kremlin in order to create what some refer to as a new world order. Private organizations such as the Council on Foreign Relations, the Royal Institute of International Affairs, the Trilateral Commission, the Dartmouth Conference, the Aspen Institute for Humanistic Studies, the Atlantic Institute, and the Bilderberg Group serve to disseminate and to coordinate the plans for this so-called new world order in powerful business, financial, academic, and official circles.

The viewpoint of the establishment today is called globalism. Not so long ago, this viewpoint was called the "one-world" view by its critics ... in the globalist point of view, nation-states and national boundaries do not count for anything. Political philosophies and political principles seem to become simply relative. Indeed, even constitutions are irrelevant to the exercise of power. Liberty and tyranny are viewed as neither necessarily good nor evil, and certainly not a component of policy.

— Senator Jesse Helms
Speech to the Senate, December 15, 1987[1]

The Council on Foreign Relations was launched in 1921 by Edward Mandell House, President Wilson's chief aide, mentor, and controller.[2] Its purpose has always been to lead our nation into world government. There has never been a more sophisticated and forceful promoter of the United Nations than this organization.

Senator Jesse Helms included the CFR in his condemnation of numerous groups working to create a "new world order," an arrangement where "nation-states and national boundaries do not count for anything." He said that, in the minds of the individuals who serve these organizations, "constitutions are irrelevant," and "liberty and tyranny are viewed as neither necessarily good nor evil." These are strong words, but there is plenty of evidence to show that they are completely merited.

Admiral Chester Ward, former Judge Advocate General of the U.S. Navy, held membership in the Council for almost 20 years. In a 1975 book he co-authored, he claimed the CFR was working for "the submergence of U.S. sovereignty and national independence into an all-powerful one-world government."

Admiral Ward further maintained that "this lust to surrender the sovereignty and independence of the United States is pervasive throughout most of the membership." And he added: "In the entire CFR lexicon, there is no term of revulsion carrying a meaning so deep as 'America First.'"[3] Wanting America to be "first" ought to be goal of any American, but it is the furthest thing from the mind of those who want world government.

If the CFR is successful, the American system will be abolished. In its place, the people of this nation will become totally subjugated to the dictates of a powerful few who plan to rule all mankind. The economic and political freedoms taken for granted in America will disappear; a forced redistribution of the wealth will bring America to her knees; and "world order" enforced by a police state will be everyone's fate.[4]

It would surely help the cause of freedom if more military officers who have been lured into CFR membership would speak out as Admiral Ward did. There ought to be many but the combination of poor understanding of the importance of preserving America's independence and an unwillingness to put aside personal ambition has kept others from following in Admiral Ward's footsteps.

Consolidating Control

In 1939, with World War II already raging in Europe, top CFR members Walter Mallory and Hamilton Fish Armstrong offered the Council's services to the State Department to aid in formulating our nation's wartime policies.

Inasmuch as the offer was made to Assistant Secretary of State George Messersmith, himself a veteran CFR member, it is no surprise that it was accepted. Thus began the formal association of our State Department and the privately run CFR.

This State Department effort became known as the War and Peace Studies Project. Like the CFR itself, it was generously funded by the Rockefeller Foundation. In subsequent years, the CFR's relationship with the State Department grew from advisory status to domination of several new State Department divisions (the Division of Special Research, the Advisory Committee on Postwar Foreign Policy, etc.).

With the appointment of CFR member Edward Stettinius as Secretary of State in 1944, the Council began to dominate our nation's foreign policy. Even during the very few occasions when the Secretary of State was not himself a CFR member, the department was always top-heavy with CFR members who were Deputy Secretaries, Under Secretaries, and Assistant Secretaries.

Secretaries of State
From 1921 to 1995

Charles Evans Hughes (CFR)	1921 – 1925
Frank B. Kellogg (CFR)	1925 – 1929
Henry L. Stimson	1929 – 1933
Cordell Hull	1933 – 1944
Edward R. Stettinius (CFR)	1944 – 1945
James F. Byrnes	1945 – 1947
George C. Marshall	1947 – 1949
Dean G. Acheson (CFR)	1949 – 1953
John Foster Dulles (CFR)	1953 – 1959

Christian A. Herter (CFR)	1959 – 1961
Dean Rusk (CFR)	1961 – 1969
William P. Rogers (CFR)	1969 – 1973
Henry A. Kissinger (CFR)	1973 – 1977
Cyrus R. Vance (CFR)	1977 – 1980
Edmund S. Muskie (CFR)	1980 – 1981
Alexander M. Haig, Jr. (CFR)	1981 – 1982
George P. Shultz (CFR)	1982 – 1989
James A. Baker, III	1989 – 1992
Lawrence S. Eagleburger (CFR)	1992 – 1993
Warren A. Christopher (CFR)	1993 – Present

In 1944, the year Edward Stettinius served as Secretary of State, there were fewer than one thousand members of the CFR. The membership has increased steadily over the years to now total a mere 3,136 persons out of the U.S. population of 260 million. Its influence on this nation, however, is immense.

There is no written law requiring that Secretaries of State must be CFR members. But there seems to be something close to one, or at least a requirement that this strategically important post must be ideologically in tune with the CFR.

CFR Targets the Military

President Roosevelt appointed CFR member Henry Stimson Secretary of War in 1940. (This post was renamed Secretary of Defense by Congress immediately after World War II.) Stimson brought CFR member John J. McCloy to Washington and named him Assistant Secretary of War in charge of personnel. In addition to later serving in numerous other government posts, McCloy would in the future be named chairman of the CFR, president of the World Bank, and chairman of the Chase Manhattan Bank. Both enemies and friends considered him the "Chairman of the Establishment."

Stimson and McCloy began a transformation within our nation's military which saw leadership of the Armed Forces pass from men who were primarily military professionals to men who could justly be classified politicians in uniform.

McCloy never sought to hide his clout, even allowing himself to be quoted by *New York Times* writer Anthony Lukas in 1971 in a revealing boast: "Whenever we needed a man, we thumbed through the roll of the Council members and put through a call to New York." Lukas added that the men McCloy recruited then called other Council members so that CFR members were soon found behind many important desks.[5]

This very same boastfulness was later expressed on March 12, 1990 by veteran CFR member and former Defense Department official Paul Nitze. Speaking at the gala opening of the CFR's new branch office in the nation's capital, he enthused about the Council's influence during the period 1920-30:

> The State Department and White House might conduct diplomacy in peace and raise and command armies in war, but policy was made by serious people, men with a longer view, that is, the great men of finance and their advisers. New York was where they were to be found.... In the postwar years, the Council has continued to represent an invaluable way for many of us Washingtonians to tap the enormously important New York business and intellectual community.[6]

By the time World War II had been won and the stage had been set for the fulfillment of the CFR's long-standing dream of a world government, CFR members knew they had enormous influence over our nation's foreign affairs. But they also knew that additional influence was needed, especially with the public at large and within the nation's military. While some CFR members targeted the public, the CFR campaign to attract and influence senior military officers began in earnest.

In 1946, U.S. Army officer Lyman L. Lemnitzer became a CFR member. He was later chosen to be Chairman of the Joint Chiefs of Staff, serving from 1960 to 1962.

In 1945, Army officer Maxwell Taylor joined the CFR. He would be recalled from retirement in 1961 and named Chairman of the

Joint Chiefs of Staff in 1962.

In 1949, retired Army officer Dwight D. Eisenhower joined the CFR. During that year, he returned to active duty and served as temporary Chairman of the Joints Chiefs of Staff. In 1950, after again retiring and again rejoining the military, he became NATO's military commander stationed in Europe. Then, from 1953 to 1961, he was President of the United States.

The following tables present a chilling picture of the CFR's domination of the top positions in our nation's military services. Most of these men accepted CFR membership while holding down the highest post in his branch. In only a few instances were these generals and admirals invited into the CFR after retirement from active military service. Beginning in the 1980s, as can be seen in the tables that follow, it was normal for the top officer of each branch of our nation's armed forces to be a CFR member.

Chairman, Joint Chiefs of Staff

Gen. Dwight D. Eisenhower (CFR)	Feb. 49 – Aug. 49
Gen. Omar N. Bradley	Aug. 49 – Aug. 53
Adm. Arthur W. Radford	Aug. 53 – Aug. 57
Gen. Nathan F. Twining	Aug. 57 – Sep. 60
Gen. Lyman L. Lemnitzer (CFR)	Oct. 60 – Sep. 62
Gen. Maxwell D. Taylor (CFR)	Oct. 62 – Jul. 64
Gen. Earle G. Wheeler	Jul. 64 – Jul. 70
Adm. Thomas H. Moorer	Jul. 74 – Jun. 78
Gen. George S. Brown	Jun. 78 – Jun. 82
Gen. David C. Jones (CFR)	Jun. 82 – Sep. 85
Gen. John W. Vessey, Jr. (CFR)	Oct. 85 – Sep. 89
Adm. William J. Crowe, Jr. (CFR)	Oct. 85 – Sep. 89
Gen. Colin L. Powell (CFR)	Oct. 89 – Sep. 93
Gen. John M. Shalikashvili*	Oct. 93 – Present

* On May 4, 1993, Gen. Shalikashvili, then the Supreme Allied Commander in Europe and the Commander in Chief of the U.S. European Command, addressed a CFR-sponsored "Roundtable Luncheon" held in San Francisco. His

Chief of Staff, U.S. Army

Gen. Dwight D. Eisenhower (CFR)	Nov. 45 – Feb. 48
Gen. Omar N. Bradley	Feb. 48 – Aug. 49
Gen. J. Lawton Collins	Aug. 49 – Aug. 53
Gen. Matthew B. Ridgway (CFR)	Aug. 53 – Jun. 55
Gen. Maxwell D. Taylor (CFR)	Jun. 55 – Jul. 59
Gen. Lyman L. Lemnitzer (CFR)	Jul. 59 – Sep. 60
Gen. George H. Decker	Oct. 60 – Sep. 62
Gen. Earle G. Wheeler	Oct. 62 – Jul. 64
Gen. Harold K. Johnson (CFR)	Jul. 64 – Jul. 68
Gen. William C. Westmoreland (CFR)	Jul. 68 – Jun. 72
Gen. Bruce Palmer, Jr.	Jul. 72 – Oct. 72
Gen. Creighton W. Abrams	Oct. 72 – Sep. 74
Gen. Fred C. Weyand	Oct. 74 – Oct. 76
Gen. Bernard W. Rogers (CFR)	Oct. 76 – Jun. 79
Gen. Edward C. Meyer	Jun. 79 – Jun. 83
Gen. John A. Wickham, Jr. (CFR)	Jun. 83 – Jun. 87
Gen. Carl E. Vuono (CFR)	Jun. 87 – Jun. 91
Gen. Gordon R. Sullivan (CFR)	Jun. 91 – Present

Chief of Staff, U.S. Air Force

Gen. Carl Spaatz	Mar. 46 – Apr. 48
Gen. Hoyt S. Vandenberg	Apr. 48 – Jun. 53
Gen. Nathan F. Twining	Jun. 53 – Jun. 57
Gen. Thomas D. White	Jul. 57 – Jun. 61
Gen. Curtis E. LeMay	Jun. 61 – Jan. 65
Gen. John P. McConnell	Feb. 65 – Aug. 69
Gen. John D. Ryan	Aug. 69 – Jul. 73
Gen. George S. Brown	Aug. 73 – Jun. 74

---

topic, as noted in the CFR's 1993 *Annual Report*, was "A New NATO For a New Era." He was following in the footsteps of other JCS chairmen who had addressed the CFR in one or more of its functions. As of September 1994, Gen. Shalikashvili is not listed as a CFR member.

Gen. David C. Jones (CFR) .... Jul. 74 – Jun. 78
Gen. Lew Allen, Jr. (CFR) .... Jul. 78 – Jun. 82
Gen. Charles A. Gabriel (CFR) .... Jul. 82 – Jun. 86
Gen. Larry D. Welch (CFR) .... Jul. 86 – Jun. 90
Gen. Michael J. Dugan (CFR) .... Jul. 90 – Sep. 90
Gen. Merrill A. McPeak (CFR) .... Oct. 90 – Oct. 94
Gen. Ronald R. Fogelman (CFR) .... Oct. 94 – Present

Commandant, U.S. Marine Corps

Gen. Lemuel C. Shepherd, Jr. .... Jun. 52 – Dec. 55
Gen. Randolph McC. Pate .... Jan. 56 – Dec. 59
Gen. David M. Shoup .... Jan. 60 – Dec. 63
Gen. Wallace M. Greene, Jr. .... Jan. 64 – Dec. 67
Gen. Leonard M. Chapman, Jr. .... Jan. 68 – Dec. 71
Gen. Robert M. Cushman, Jr. .... Jan. 72 – Jun. 75
Gen. Louis A. Wilson .... Jul. 75 – Jun. 79
Gen. Robert H. Barrow .... Jul. 79 – Jun. 83
Gen. Paul X. Kelley (CFR) .... Jul. 83 – Jun. 87
Gen. Alfred M. Gray, Jr. .... Jul. 87 – Jul. 91
Gen. Carl E. Mundy, Jr. (CFR) .... Jul. 91 – Present

Chief of Naval Operations

Adm. Chester W. Nimitz .... Dec. 45 – Dec. 47
Adm. Louis E. Denfield .... Dec. 47 – Nov. 49
Adm. Forrest P. Sherman .... Nov. 49 – Jul. 51
Adm. William M. Fechteler .... Aug. 51 – Aug. 53
Adm. Robert B. Carney .... Aug. 53 – Aug. 55
Adm. Arleigh B. Burke .... Aug. 55 – Aug. 61
Adm. George W. Anderson, Jr. (CFR) .... Aug. 61 – Aug. 63
Adm. David L. McDonald .... Aug. 63 – Aug. 67
Adm. Thomas H. Moorer .... Aug. 67 – Jul. 70
Adm. Elmo R. Zumwalt, Jr. (CFR) .... Jul. 70 – Jul. 74

Adm. James L. Holloway III .... Jul. 74 – Jul. 78
Adm. Thomas B. Hayward (CFR) .... Jul. 78 – Jul. 82
Adm. James D. Watkins .... Jul. 82 – Jul. 86
Adm. Carlisle A.H. Trost (CFR) .... Jul. 86 – Jun. 90
Adm. Frank B. Kelso II .... Jul. 90 – Present

Secretary of Defense

James V. Forrestal .... Sep. 47 – Mar. 49*
Louis A. Johnson .... Sep. 49 – Sep. 50
George C. Marshall .... Sep. 50 – Sep. 51
Robert V. Lovett (CFR) .... Sep. 51 – Jan. 53
Charles E. Wilson .... Jan. 53 – Oct. 57
Neil H. McElroy (CFR) .... Oct. 57 – Dec. 59
Thomas S. Gates, Jr. (CFR) .... Dec. 59 – Jan. 61
Robert S. McNamara (CFR) .... Jan. 61 – Feb. 68
Clark M. Clifford .... Mar. 68 – Jan. 69
Melvin R. Laird (CFR) .... Jan. 69 – Jan. 73
Elliott L. Richardson (CFR) .... Jan. 73 – May 73
James R. Schlesinger (CFR) .... Jul. 73 – Nov. 75
Donald H. Rumsfeld (CFR) .... Nov. 75 – Jan. 77
Harold Brown (CFR) .... Jan. 77 – Jan. 81
Caspar Weinberger (CFR) .... Jan. 81 – Nov. 87
Frank C. Carlucci (CFR) .... Nov. 87 – Jan. 89
Richard B. Cheney (CFR) .... Mar. 89 – Jan. 93
Les Aspin (CFR) .... Jan. 93 – Feb. 94†
William Perry .... Feb. 94 – Present

* James Forrestal held CFR membership from 1924 to 1931. He had long separated himself from the organization when he accepted appointment as Secretary of Defense.

† Former Congressman Les Aspin told senators during his confirmation hearings: "The President is the Commander in Chief.... Congress has war powers. If you second these forces to the UN, how do you maintain the Constitution?" Aspin's attitude about the importance of the Constitution could have marked him for early retirement.

National Security Adviser (Since 1960)

McGeorge Bundy (CFR)
Walt W. Rostow (CFR)
Henry A. Kissinger (CFR)
Brent Scowcroft (CFR)
Zbigniew Brzezinski (CFR)
Richard V. Allen
William P. Clark
Robert C. McFarlane (CFR)
John M. Poindexter
Frank C. Carlucci (CFR)
Colin Powell (CFR)
Brent Scowcroft (CFR)
W. Anthony Lake (CFR)

Director of Central Intelligence (Since 1950)

Walter Bedell Smith (CFR)
Allen Dulles (CFR)
John A. McCone
William F. Raborn, Jr.
Richard Helms (CFR)
James R. Schlesinger (CFR)
William E. Colby (CFR)
George Bush (CFR)
Stansfield Turner (CFR)
William Casey (CFR)
William Webster (CFR)
Robert Gates (CFR)
R. James Woolsey (CFR)

CFR Military Fellows

In 1962, the CFR launched its Military Fellows Program. Senior officers (colonels or navy captains) were assigned by their respective branches to spend an entire year at CFR headquarters in New York City. The purpose of the program, as described by the CFR, "is to allow the fellows to broaden their interest and knowledge of foreign policy by following their own intellectual pursuits and participating in Council activities." They also pitch in to help the CFR produce "studies" in the fields of diplomacy and foreign affairs.

After a year at CFR headquarters, most of these men found promotion to general or admiral rather routine. Some even found themselves invited into CFR membership.

Air Force Colonel Marshall Sanders was the first fellow during 1962-63. The second, Air Force Colonel Robert Ginsburgh, spent 1963-64 at the Harold Pratt House (CFR headquarters). His acceptance of Council membership in 1965 likely sped his promotion to Brigadier General and then to Major General. His name appeared on the CFR membership roster for the next 26 years.

Dr. Susan L.M. Huck questioned General Ginsburgh about his unusual tour of duty and reported his attitude in the October 1977 issue of *American Opinion* magazine. Ginsburgh told her:

> The Air Force, as an instrument of national policy, ought to be aware of what people of importance are thinking about. [The CFR's program] is a useful way of educating outstanding Air Force officers who are expected to be in leadership and management positions to have a feel for the way the country was headed.[7]

Precisely! The CFR will fill the heads of selected military men with the "way the country was headed." Of course, CFR members serving as Presidents and as the leaders of the State, Defense, Treasury, and other departments of government are the very individuals who decide which way the country is to be "headed." The Military Fellows program assures that some of the best brains in the military acquiesce with what is being done to America, and it also results in having these men spread the word about how brilliantly the nation was being directed.

Ginsburgh agreed that anyone who spent a year at the CFR

would find promotion more likely. Speaking of those who make such promotion selections, he said of a tour of duty at CFR headquarters, "People know what it means." Yes, they do. And the word soon spread within the military services that the CFR Military Fellows program is a ticket to higher rank. An ambitious participant in this program would certainly not call attention to the brainwashing it entails, nor would he find it in his personal best interests to challenge the top-heavy presence of CFR members in high military posts.

In 1980, after retiring from active duty, Ginsburgh began serving the CFR as a member of its nominating committee choosing officers to be Military Fellows. His colleagues on this panel included two other CFR members, retired General Lyman Lemnitzer and retired Admiral John M. Lee.

Here is a complete listing of all CFR Military Fellows from the very beginning of this little-known program:

1962 – 63	AF	Col. Marshall Sanders
1963 – 64	AF	Col. Robert N. Ginsburgh (joined CFR 1965)
1964 – 65	AF	Col. Edward Foote
1965 – 66	AF	Col. Immanuel Klette
1966 – 67	AF	Col. Frederick Thayer
	Army	Col. Michael Greene
1967 – 68	AF	Col. Kemper Baker
	Army	Col. Sidney Berry (joined CFR 1970, future Superintendent at West Point)
1968 – 69	Army	Col. Sam Walker
	Navy	Capt. Robert Welander
1969 – 70	AF	Col. George Loving
	Navy	Capt. Charles Tesh
1970 – 71	AF	Col. William Usher
	Army	Col. Robert Gard (joined CFR 1971)
1971 – 72	Army	Col. James Thompson
	Navy	Capt. John Dewenter
1972 – 73	AF	Col. Leon Pfeiffer
	Navy	Capt. Robert Miale

1973 – 74	AF	Col. Thomas Julian
	Army	Col. Thomas Ayers
1974 – 75	AF	Col. James Pfautz
	Navy	Capt. Stewart Ring
1975 – 76	AF	Col. Merrill McPeak (joined CFR 1989, future AF Chief of Staff 1990)
	Army	Col. Arthur Dewey
1976 – 77	AF	Col. John Wolcott
	Navy	Capt. Harry Fiske
1977 – 78	AF	Col. Richard Head
	Army	Col. John Sewall
1978 – 79	Army	Col. Zeb B. Bradford, Jr.
	Navy	Capt. Howland J. Kerr
1979 – 80	Army	Col. Bernard Loeffke
	Navy	Capt. Ronald J. Kurth
1980 – 81	AF	Col. Jeffery A. Levy
1981 – 82	Navy	Capt. Donald O. Gentry
	AF	Col. Thomas E. Eggers
1982 – 83	USMC	Col. Matthew P. Caulfield (joined CFR 1991)
	Army	Col. Timothy J. Grogan
1983 – 84	Army	Col. Thomas H. Harvey
	AF	Col. Dale E. Stovall
1984 – 85	Army	Col. David Cooper
	AF	Col. K. Scott Fisher
1985 – 86	Navy	Capt. Barry M. Plott
	AF	Col. Bruce M. Freeman
1986 – 87	USMC	Col. Philip M. Harrington
	AF	Col. Donald E. Loranger (Joined CFR 1992)
1987 – 88	Army	Col. Stanley Kwieciak
1988 – 89	Navy	Capt. A.K. Cebrowski
	AF	Col. Jamie Gough III
	Army	Col. Francis P. Keogh
1989 – 90	Navy	Capt. Edward Charles Long III
	AF	Col. Thomas H. Neary
1990 – 91	AF	Col. William M. Drennan, Jr.
	USMC	Col. Wallace C. Gregson

	Army	Col. Jack B. Wood
1991 – 92	USMC	Col. David M. Mize
	Army	Col. John P. Rose
1992 – 93	Army	Col. Daniel R. Zanini
	AF	Col. Maxwell C. Bailey
1993 – 94	USMC	Col. Stephen A. Cheney
	Army	Col. L. Patrick Wright
1994 – 95	AF	Col. John R. Baker
	Army	Col. Burwell B. Bell
	USMC	Col. Larry D. Outlaw

With very few exceptions, these men were later promoted to general or admiral rank. The Military Fellows Program is one of the CFR's great successes.

CFR Reaches Out for Others

Through its Military Fellows Program, the CFR has succeeded in planting its internationalist and anti-independence thinking into the minds of many military officers. Not only those who spent a year at CFR headquarters were affected; many who see promotions speedily achieved by participants in this program have adapted their own thinking to coincide with CFR attitudes.

But the CFR hasn't confined its penetration of the military merely to its Military Fellows program alone. The organization has continually reached out to gather other senior officers under its wing by extending membership each year to high-ranking military personnel. We took a look at a ten-year period beginning in 1978. Many of these men have risen to positions at the very top levels of the armed services.

— 1978 —

Vice Adm. B.R. Inman, USN (future Deputy Director of the CIA, nominated to be Secretary of Defense in 1993 but mysteriously withdrew his name after expressing delight at being chosen)

Col. William E. Odom, U.S. Army

Col. George K. Osborn, U.S. Army
Lt. Gen. William Y. Smith, USAF
Rear Adm. Carlisle A. H. Trost, USN (future Chief of Naval Operations)

— 1979 —

Vice Adm. William J. Crowe, USN (future Chief of Naval Operations, U.S. Ambassador to England)
Vice Adm. Thor Hanson, USN
Gen. Edward C. Meyer, U.S. Army
Gen. John A. Wickham, U.S. Army (future Army Chief of Staff)

— 1980 —

Gen. David C. Jones, USAF (future Air Force Chief of Staff)
Capt. Gary G. Sick, USN

— 1981 —

Gen. Lew Allen, USAF (future Air Force Chief of Staff)
Maj. Gen. Jack N. Merritt, U.S. Army

— 1982 —

Vice Adm. S.R. Foley, Jr., USN
Vice Adm. M. Staser Holcomb, USN
Lt. Gen. William R. Richardson, U.S. Army
Adm. Harry D. Train, USN
Gen. John W. Vessey, U.S. Army (future Army Chief of Staff)
Lt. Col. Edward C. Warner, USAF

— 1983 —

Col. George Lee Butler, USAF
Lt. Col. Wesley K. Clark, U.S. Army
Gen. Charles A. Gabriel, USAF (future AF Chief of Staff)
Lt. Col. James R. Golden, U.S. Army
Gen. P.X. Kelley, USMC (future Marine Corps Commandant)

Gen. Bernard W. Rogers, U.S. Army (future Army Chief of Staff)
Lt. Gen. M.R. Thurman, U.S. Army

— 1984 —

Lt. Gen. John T. Chain, USAF
Gen. James E. Dalton, USAF
Adm. Thomas B. Hayward, USN (future Chief of Naval Operations)
Col. Frank B. Horton III, USAF
Lt. Gen. Fred K. Mahaffey, U.S. Army
Lt. Cdr. James G. Stavridis, USN
Lt. Gen. Bernard E. Trainor, USMC (future Harvard University faculty member)

— 1985 —

Lt. Gen. Richard D. Lawrence, U.S. Army
Brig. Gen. Ervin J. Rokke, USAF

— 1986 —

Brig. Gen. Ronald R. Fogleman, USAF
Lt. Gen. Colin L. Powell, U.S. Army (future Chairman, Joint Chiefs of Staff)
Lt. Col. Norton A. Schwartz, USAF

— 1987 —

Maj. Gen. Marcus Anderson, USAF

— 1988 —

Gen. John R. Galvin, U.S. Army (future NATO Commander)
Gen. Carl E. Vuono, U.S. Army (future Army Chief of Staff)

Another tactic employed by the CFR to gain influence within the military involves having CFR members placed as the leaders of the nation's service academies.

At West Point, seven superintendents have been CFR members

during the past 50 years. It is likely that cadets in training have been affected by the thinking of CFR members who led the academy. The CFR members who have served as superintendent at West Point are:

Gen. Maxwell Taylor (CFR) .... 1945 – 49
Gen. William C. Westmoreland (CFR) .... 1960 – 63
Gen. Lames P. Lampert (CFR) .... 1963 – 66
Gen. Donald V. Bennett (CFR) .... 1966 – 68
Gen. William A. Knowlton (CFR) .... 1970 – 74
Gen. Sidney B. Berry (CFR) .... 1974 – 77
Gen. Andrew J. Goodpaster (CFR) .... 1977 – 81
Gen. Howard D. Graves (CFR) .... 1991 – Present

Also, Air Force Lieutenant General Bradley Hosmer (CFR) served as Superintendent of the U.S. Air Force Academy from June 1991 to June 1994. Rear Admiral Charles R. Larson (CFR) held the post of Superintendent of the U.S. Naval Academy from August 1983 to August 1986, and was reappointed to the position after being promoted to full Admiral in August 1994.

CFR Meetings and Programs

A sizeable number of the CFR's programs, meetings, conferences, and seminars have been specifically directed toward the military. Some are even conducted by high-ranking military officers who are members of the Council.

Many other meetings, of course, present the views of high-ranking U.S. government officials and their counterparts from other nations. Military personnel who attend these sessions come away with the perspectives presented by and acceptable to the CFR. Important alternative perspectives, of course, receive no airing whatsoever at CFR meetings.

We list some of the CFR's sessions dealing specifically with military matters and featuring military personnel during only two recent one-year periods even though this type activity occurs every year.

September 1989 – June 1990

October 10, 1989: The CFR conducted a seminar for the students of the U.S. Army War College.

December 7, 1989: Air Force General Larry D. Welch (CFR) addressed a CFR Roundtable Luncheon on the topic, "Adjusting to World Change: A Report From the U.S. Air Force."

January 18, 1990: Army General John R. Galvin (CFR) addressed a CFR Roundtable Dinner on the topic, "The North Atlantic Alliance: Managing Change."

February 20, 1990: Air Force General Michael Dugan (CFR) addressed a CFR Roundtable Luncheon on the topic, "Change and the European Security Environment."

April 16, 1990: The CFR organized a meeting for members at the Pentagon with the entire membership of the Joint Chiefs of Staff.

April 21 – 28, 1990: The CFR organized a trip for members to NATO headquarters and installations in Europe.

April 23, 1990: Army General Colin L. Powell (CFR) addressed a CFR General Meeting held in Washington on the topic, "U.S. Foreign Policy in a Changing World."

September 1993 – June 1994

September 8, 1993: Army General John M. Shalikashvili addressed a General Luncheon on the topic, "NATO: Still Worth the Effort?"

October 12, 1993: The CFR conducted a seminar for the students of the U.S. Army War College.

October 12, 1993: Admiral Paul David Miller (CFR) delivered a seminar program at the Washington CFR center entitled, "The American Military: The Dynamics of Change."

March 6 – 9, 1994: The CFR organized a trip for its members to the Marine Corps base at Twentynine Palms, California; the Army base at Fort Irwin, California; and the National Training

Command at Nellis Air Force Base, Las Vegas, Nevada.

March 16, 1994: Army General Gordon R. Sullivan (CFR) addressed a General Luncheon on the topic, "Building a 21st Century Army."

April 10 – 16, 1994: The CFR organized a visit for members to NATO headquarters in Brussels, Belgium; the U.S. Air Force installation in Naples, Italy; and the detachment of U.S. military personnel serving in the United Nations Protection Force (UNPROFOR) in Macedonia.

May 23, 1994: The CFR organized a visit for members with Joint Chiefs of Staff Chairman General John M. Shalikashvili at his Pentagon office.

The Constitution

Every member of the armed forces swears an oath to uphold the U.S. Constitution. Yet, any study of both the CFR and the Constitution shows very clearly their incompatibility. Anyone who is loyal to one cannot be loyal to the other. But no one in our nation's military has sworn any oath to the CFR, so the choice of which should be adhered to ought to be eminently clear.

A major problem, however, is that the full meaning of the Constitution is little understood. Military officers who have affiliated with the Council will insist that they have not compromised themselves and that they certainly are not violating their oath or betraying their nation. They do not believe their CFR membership and their CFR-induced attitudes conflict with the Constitution because they have little or no appreciation of what the document means. And besides, many would say, the President, many cabinet officers, and many high-ranking military officers are CFR members. How can anything be wrong with the CFR?

Most of the military officers who have affiliated with the CFR are not conspirators; they are the Conspiracy's unwitting and dutiful servants. But the nation itself will be the Conspiracy's certain victim if CFR plans aren't thwarted.

We have never contended that all who hold CFR membership are knowing and willing destroyers of this nation. But there is no doubt about the destructive purpose of this organization. Many otherwise intelligent and well-meaning military professionals have been drawn into the CFR and are being used to further its designs.

Let us, therefore, issue a challenge to any military officer one who has been flattered into accepting CFR membership and the CFR's perspectives: Study the history and underlying purpose of this group; relearn the full meaning of the U.S. Constitution; refuse to be a pawn in the CFRs deadly game; lend your voice to the growing number of Americans who have become aware of the subversion in our midst; and steer your efforts toward restoring America's principles, not compromising them on the altar of world government.

In short, stand by your oath. If you do and choose to become another Admiral Chester Ward, you will have earned the thanks of your loyal countrymen.

The Military Oath

I do solemnly swear that I will support and defend the Constitution of the United States against all enemies foreign and domestic; that I will bear true faith and allegiance to the same; that I take this obligation freely, without any mental reservation or purpose of evasion; that I will well and faithfully discharge the duties of the office on which I am about to enter; so help me God.

CHAPTER 12

POW Abandonment Affects Morale

From what I have witnessed, it appears that any soldier left in Vietnam, even inadvertently, was, in fact, abandoned years ago, and that the farce that is being played is no more than political legerdemain done with "smoke and mirrors" to stall the issue until it dies a natural death.

— Colonel Millard A. Peck, U.S. Army
February 12, 1991[1]

No discussion of the POW/MIA topic should fail to acknowledge the immense heartache and frustration endured by thousands of family members. When the Vietnam War ended, there was reason to believe that as many as 5,000 captured Americans would be returned.[2] But the North Vietnamese delivered only 591 during "Operation Homecoming," February 12 to March 29, 1973.

In Vietnam, our government failed our POWs and MIAs, and there is plenty of evidence to suggest that the failure was deliberate. The cost in morale throughout the military has been enormous. But what is even worse is the realization that leaders who will betray their men in uniform will also betray the nation itself.

Colonel Peck's Resignation

Colonel Millard A. Peck was a soldier's soldier. His distinguished Army career saw him serve three combat tours in Vietnam. He earned a chest full of medals and commendations including the nation's second highest award, the Distinguished Service Cross.

In mid-1990, Peck *volunteered* to serve as chief of the Defense Intelligence Agency's Special Office for Prisoners of War. He knew what he was getting into, later acknowledging his awareness that the job was "highly contentious and extremely frustrating." But it would be worth all of its trials, he felt, if he could get some answers — and maybe get some more POWs and MIAs home.

After eight months of utter frustration, however, he tacked a letter asking to be relieved of his duties to the door of his office and walked away. The letter said he did not want to be a part of "coverup." It claimed that most of those directing the nation's POW/MIA program had a "mindset to debunk" reports of sightings coming out of Southeast Asia and that the entire effort amounted to a "charade" filled with "high-level knavery." He also stated:

> That National leaders continue to address the prisoner of war and missing in action issue as the "highest national priority" is a travesty....
>
> From what I have witnessed, it appears that any soldier left in Vietnam, even inadvertently, was, in fact, abandoned years ago, and that the farce that is being played is no more than political legerdemain done with "smoke and mirrors" to stall the issue until it dies a natural death.

Peck did not run to the press with his resignation and its stinging assessments. Hardly anyone knew what he had done until just prior to his appearance before the House Foreign Affairs Subcommittee on Asian and Pacific Affairs. On May 30, 1991, he provided the subcommittee with "new information," including names of officials who impeded the effort to resolve the POW/MIA situation.

Immediately, Peck found his information discounted and himself discredited by those above and around him. But he was not the first to arrive at such conclusions or to receive such treatment. Unfortunately, his conclusions square with facts that have surfaced over many years.

Betrayal Begun by Nixon and Kissinger

On January 27, 1973, our nation's chief negotiator at the Paris Peace Conference, Henry Kissinger, joined with the representatives of North Vietnam, South Vietnam, and the South Vietnam Provisional Revolutionary Government in signing an agreement to end the war. Our side found itself dealing from a position of weakness brought on by the no-win policies governing how our forces fought the war. Had we achieved victory, we could have dictated the terms. But because we had announced plans to pull out without victory, we were made to accept the terms of others.

In addition, our adversaries were surely in league with the large civilian anti-war movement here at home. North Vietnam's leaders knew that actress Jane Fonda* and others had actually visited with them in Hanoi while the forces under their command were killing Americans in the rice paddies and jungles to the south. And they were certainly aware of the declining public and political support for the war in the U.S. Congress.

Article 21 of the January 27, 1973 peace agreement contained a U.S. pledge to "contribute to healing the wounds of war and to post-war reconstruction of the Democratic Republic of Vietnam and throughout Indo-China." Further along, the pact stated that the return of POWs would be "carried out simultaneously with and completed not later than the same day as the troop withdrawal."

But the North Vietnamese produced no list of POWs until after the accord was signed, meaning our negotiators had put themselves into a position where they were given no choice but to accept at a later date whatever the enemy produced by way of men or lists of names.

Eventually a list was produced, and it contained the names of only nine Americans who had been captured in Laos and transferred to North Vietnam. There was solid evidence that as many as 100 men lost in Laos were still alive, all of whom were sup-

---

* Fonda was photographed in North Vietnam smilingly sitting at an anti-aircraft weapon of the type being used to shoot down American planes.

posed to be returned by the North Vietnamese.* State Department officials had contended that the list of nine names provided by the North Vietnamese in cooperation with the Pathet Lao "was incomplete."[3] And a Pathet Lao spokesman himself had admitted that his forces were indeed retaining other Americans.†

The last repatriation of Americans occurred on March 29th. Two days earlier, a North Vietnamese spokesman stated that any U.S. demand that prisoners captured in Laos must be released by his country "was beyond the jurisdiction of the [Paris] agreement." No more POWs from Laos have ever been returned. They were forgotten by Kissinger and his team. In fact, no more POWs from anywhere else in Southeast Asia came home after March 29, 1973.

When the peace accord was signed on January 27, 1973, the Department of Defense listed a total of 2,383 personnel unaccounted for (1,259 POW/MIAs, and 1,124 killed in action/body not recovered). But, as we stated previously, only 591 were released even though our own government had, in other places, demanded the return of 5,000.[4]

There were plenty of reasons to demand more returnees and more accountability. Yet, on April 13, 1973, the Department of Defense issued a formal statement claiming:

> There are no more prisoners in Southeast Asia. They are all dead.

And the very next day saw the launching in Washington of the official line insisting that any further claim about men still being alive in Southeast "does the families a disservice." President Nixon quickly added his voice to the "all dead" assertion when he stated in a speech on May 19, 1973:

---

* A UPI dispatch from Vientiane, Laos on March 25, 1973 stated: "U.S. sources believe that a substantial number of the missing [in Laos] — perhaps as many as 100 — still may be alive."

† A UPI dispatch from Vientiane on February 19, 1973 stated that "a Communist Pathet Lao spokesman" publicly announced that "his group is holding American prisoners of war."

For the first time in 12 years, we can observe Armed Forces Day with all of our fighting forces home from Vietnam and all of our courageous prisoners of war set free and here back home in America.

But reports indicting that Americans had been seen in Southeast Asia continued to arrive in a steady stream. By 1991, the Defense Department had accumulated 11,700 such reports claiming that missing men were still alive. Of these, 1,400 were first-hand, live sightings of Americans. All of the evidence in these reports has been closed to the press, the families, and POW organizations. Amazingly, it was not closed to North Vietnam's officials according to Colonel Peck, who received orders to give everything he had to the communist government in Hanoi. Peck was asked about this incredible turn of events by Faith Daniels of NBC's *Today* program on August 5, 1991:

Daniels: You were ordered to hand over all your documentation and procedures of investigations to Hanoi?

Peck: That's true.

Daniels: Why would they do that? Why would they tell you to give all that to our former enemy?

Peck: The rationale that was given at the time — I thought it was very spurious logic — was if we can gain a measure of trust and if we can prove to the Vietnamese that we're honest, open, forthcoming, and that we're really nice guys, they will reciprocate....

Daniels: Instead we gave them the ability to sort of answer all the questions without really getting to the bottom of anything.

Peck: That's exactly what I thought....

Daniels: Wouldn't Hanoi have something to gain by handing over POWs if it's still holding them?

Peck: No, I don't think they would do that. I think their rationale is to hold these people as bargaining chips, because that's the only collateral they have. That's the one thing ... they can always put out on a bargaining table that will ensure the United States returns.... When they no longer feel that they need them — when they get such things as aid, trade, recognition, World Bank loans, a seat in the UN — they have no more need for hostages; they have no more need to bring the United States back to the bargaining table. They can get rid of these guys.

Daniels: Kill them?

Peck: Yes, I think it would be embarrassing for the regime to all of a sudden, once they get everything they want, to release a number of POWs back to the United States. I don't think the American people would stand for it.[5]

It is easy to understand how the winners of this war would want to continue punishing our nation as much as they dare. But what was not known to virtually anyone but President Nixon and Kissinger is that the Vietnamese were conducting their side of the negotiations based in large part on a secret promise for reparations made to them by Kissinger only days after the signing of the peace accord.

President Nixon's Letter

On February 1, 1973, Henry Kissinger hand carried a letter from the President to North Vietnam's Prime Minister. It contained specific details about our nation's plans to "contribute to healing the wounds of war and to post-war reconstruction," as mentioned in Article 21 of the peace accord then being hammered out. But the very existence of this letter was not revealed to Congress or the press until five years later when some of our negotiators were shown it in Hanoi.

The letter called for the U.S. to provide as much as "$3.25 billion of grant aid over five years," and "other forms of aid ... in the range of 1 to 1.5 billion dollars." And it contained our government's pledge to create a U.S.- Vietnam Joint Economic Commission to develop "economic, trade and other relations" between the two countries.[6]

Neither Kissinger nor the President could deliver the funds they had promised without gaining congressional approval. But Congress already considered any such funding the equivalent of reparations or tribute, the price only a guilty party would pay.

And Congress was in no mood to admit that our nation had incurred any guilt in the war. Also, a citizen campaign against "reparations" strengthened the will of Congress.*

Adding further to the sentiment against supplying funds to North Vietnam were the horrifying tales of torture and abuse suffered by returning POWs. Practically all were savaged while in the hands of the North Vietnamese.†

On April 6, 1973, the U.S. Senate voted 88-3 against providing aid to North Vietnam. Less than a week later, House Armed Services Chairman F. Edward Hebert (D-LA) announced that he would introduce a bill in the House to complement the Senate's action. There was no way Congress would agree to give North Vietnam any money.

With near unanimous congressional resistance to aid, and with the cancellation of the 1964 embargo prohibiting U.S. companies from doing business with North Vietnam also virtually unanimous, the Department of Defense responded with the aforementioned April 13th announcement: "There are no more prisoners in Southeast Asia. They are all dead." One day later, a government spokesman promulgated what would become official policy, that spreading any "rumors" about missing men still being alive did the families a "disservice." In effect, our own government had given the North Vietnamese every reason to do away with the men they were holding since their value as hostages for reparations had evaporated.

From then until now, Administration after Administration has held fast to the attitude, "They are all dead." There has been

---

* This campaign, launched by The John Birch Society, employed the slogan "Not One RED Cent!"

† One of the most compelling accounts of both the horror of being a POW and the bravery of a man who endured six years in captivity can be found in *Scars and Stripes* by Navy Captain Eugene B. "Red" McDaniel. Not content with his joy over returning to the United States, Captain McDaniel has become a leading crusader for the cause of other POW/MIAs through the group he serves as President: American Defense Institute, 1055 North Fairfax Street, Alexandria, VA 22314.

plenty of paper shuffling and lots of talk from the State Department, Defense Department, and other government agencies, but no action of any substance. After all, why should a government insisting that all these men are "dead" put any real effort into rescuing them?

Five years later, in September 1978, when the issue would not go away because of the steady stream of reports about Americans being seen in the former war zone, a House Special Committee on Southeast Asia called Under Secretary of State Philip Habib to testify. Asked by Representative Benjamin Gilman (R-NY) if he knew of any "agreements we are not aware of, secret memorandums that this committee is not aware of," Habib responded, "There is no agreement or secret memorandum...."

A somewhat piqued Representative Frank McCloskey (D-IN) immediately jumped in to ask Habib:

> With all due respect, Mr. Secretary, this committee asked the Secretary of State and you the same question before we went to Hanoi last December. You did not advise us of that secret [Kissinger hand-carried] letter and *we discovered its existence only when we got to Hanoi....* We didn't have any idea the letter existed. We asked you in November if there were any secret agreements that we should know about before we went to Hanoi and we were not advised by you or the Secretary of State of the letter's existence or of the $3.25 billion figure which we later ascertained. [Emphasis added]

Habib's amazing response was, "That [the letter] is not an agreement. It never developed into an agreement. *I didn't know of the existence of the letter ... either.*"[7] [Emphasis added.]

In no way do we intend to minimize the brutality suffered by the POWs or the inhumanity of the North Vietnamese who failed to return most of them. But the officials in Hanoi were holding a written promise that they would receive billions in aid from the U.S. That promise had not been given by a low-level government functionary; it came in a letter from President Nixon delivered in person by his top envoy.

As their own way of guaranteeing that the pledge of aid given by men they did not trust might be honored, they held on to many of the Americans. Such a barbaric policy was nothing new for the Vietnamese communists. It was well known that they had returned only 11,000 of 39,000 French POWs when their war with France ended in France's defeat at Dienbienphu in 1954.

Both the President and Kissinger kept quiet about their pledge to the North Vietnamese and their inability to deliver the promised aid, thus sealing the fate of POWs held in Vietnam. As soon as it was obvious to Mr. Nixon and his top envoy that Congress was not going to produce the aid package, the State Department issued the "They are all dead" statement. At that point, any men who were still alive were effectively abandoned.

It was bad enough that President Nixon, Kissinger, and others had directed the war in such a way that many of our men were taken prisoner. But they made their dark deeds even darker with the way they sealed the fate of most of the POWs.

Men Were Known to Be Alive

During 1974-75, Army Colonel John H. Madison Jr. served as the leader of the U.S. section of a Four-Party Joint Military Team (the U.S., South Vietnam, North Vietnam, and Viet Cong) formed to account for American POWs and MIAs. In comments appearing in the March 1992 issue of *The American Legion* magazine, this now-retired senior officer stated of the Vietnamese:

> They are still hanging on to the idea that we are going to give them some money. When the Four-Party Joint Military Team used to go up to Hanoi — we went up there every Friday on a liaison flight in a U.S. Air Force C-130 — the North Vietnamese would point out this rail yard on the north side of the Red River.
>
> It was completely cut out by the B-52s Christmas raid of 1972. And they told me that "when you people give us the money to fix this, we might give you some information on your POW/MIAs."
>
> POW/MIA information during the Vietnam War was consolidated at the Hanoi level and is in a file cabinet there. And they will give it

> to us in drips and drabs or all at once depending on when they get ready. Certainly, they know a great deal more about POW/MIAs than they've told the United States.[8]

Army Lieutenant Colonel Stuart A. Harrington is another of many who added confirmation that men were alive and should not have been abandoned. During 1973-75, he served as our nation's military intelligence and liaison officer dealing with the North Vietnamese and representatives of the Peoples Republic of China. In his 1983 book entitled *Peace With Honor? An American Reports on Vietnam, 1973-1975*, Harrington revealed that North Vietnamese officials freely admitted to him that POWs would be returned after the Americans produced the promised aid. He wrote:

> U.S. casualties under North Vietnamese control would be accounted for and prisoners returned after fulfillment of the promise.[9]

On June 25, 1981, Lieutenant General Eugene Tighe, former director of the Defense Intelligence Agency (DIA), testified before Congress about Americans being forsaken. He repeated his beliefs in 1986, stating: "A large volume of evidence leads to the conclusion that POWs are still alive." Former North Carolina Congressman Bill Hendon said of Tighe that DIA officials "bugged his office,... made him change his report, and marked it secret."

Tighe's report was dug out years later by Senator Bob Smith (R-NH). Tighe claimed that upwards of 90 percent of the refugee live-sightings were credible even though he admitted having publicly classified some live-sighting reports as unreliable "for fear that if the Hanoi government knew I was looking into a specific sighting in a specific place at a specific time, they might get there first."[10]

The 1991 Republican Staff Report of the Senate Foreign Relations Committee, from which we have drawn a great deal of our information, concluded its discussion of this sordid abandonment of our men with a relatively temperate summation. It states:

> Perhaps if Congress and the American public had known of the existence of the secret letter, perhaps if Congress had been given a full accounting of the information on MIAs possessed by the U.S. government, instead of a cover-up, then a concrete plan for implementing the provisions for gaining accounting of captives, as described in the Paris Peace Accords, might have been implemented. But there was no way that Congress, with honor, could be blackmailed into accepting the payment of reparations with its tacit implication of surrender to a ruthless Communist regime.[11]

What happened because of that secret Kissinger letter to POWs who were still alive and never came home deserves a more direct comment. We offer the following:

> If Mr. Nixon and Mr. Kissinger had informed Congress and the American people about their secret promises, if they had claimed that fulfilling them was the surest and best way of getting POWs back and obtaining a reliable listing of those who had died, and if they had just been completely honest about what they had done, *it seems certain that many more Americans would have made it home.*

Further, if the information provided to the government over the past 20 years — especially what is contained in the 1,400 first-hand live-sighting reports — had been acted upon instead of been the object of furious debunking efforts, more Americans might have come home. With the exception of a minuscule few of these sightings designated "unresolved," the Department of Defense has concluded that such reports are not credible and do not provide any worthwhile information about missing Americans.

According to Colonel Peck, every time one of these reports reached the appropriate office, government personnel conducted a "damage limitation exercise" consisting mainly of "finding fault with the source." While government officials continued to protest that resolving the POW/MIA situation was their "highest national priority," the truth is that coverup was far more important to them. Because higher-ups had insisted "They are all dead," backing that attitude up became their all-consuming task.

In his resignation letter, Colonel Peck even issued sharp criticism of Ann Mills Griffiths and her leadership of the National League of Families, the organization supposedly acting on behalf of bereaved family members still hoping that their men might be returned. Peck never used the word "conspiracy," but what he wrote surely implied that one existed. In one of his six conclusions critical of Mills and the League, Peck stated:

> National League of Families: I am convinced that the Director of this organization is much more than meets the eye. As the principal actor in the grand show, she is in the perfect position to clamor for "progress", while really intentionally impeding the effort. And there are numerous examples of this. Otherwise it is inconceivable that so many bureaucrats in the "system" would instantaneously do her bidding and humor her every whim.[12]

During the summer of 1992, President Bush addressed a POW/MIA convention in Washington. When his defense of the unconscionable government position proved too much for some listeners, he was jeered by family members. He lost his temper and told these desperate people to "Sit down and shut up!"

Undoubtedly, there are family members who have studied this matter in great detail for more than 20 years. They know as much about the government's coverup as anyone. They do not intend to let an opportunity to express their disgust pass quietly because they know the government is covering up and they are not about to listen to more prevarications, no matter who issues them.

They also know what Colonel Peck has stated. They know General Tighe's attitude. And they also know about the Garwood case.

In 1973, a live-sighting report about Marine Private Robert Garwood reached the Department of Defense. It was discounted because "They are all dead" had become official policy. But Garwood surfaced and made it back to the United States in 1979. He was immediately court-martialed as a deserter and collaborator, thus solving two problems for the Department of Defense: 1)

As a deserter, he could not be considered a POW and could not be cited as evidence of the wrongness of the "They are all dead" claim; and 2) a huge percentage of live-sightings were immediately declared to have been of Garwood and were summarily dismissed as "solved."

The reason for Garwood having been in Vietnamese hands for many years is far less important than the fact that he came home. Once back in the U.S., he provided "live-sighting" reports about 30 Americans he had seen in the years since the government had proclaimed them all "dead." His testimony should have been acted upon, not filed and discounted along with many hundreds of other reports. But it was not.

Government officials solved their own Garwood problem with his court martial, and the POWs remained "dead." The government that quickly labeled this man a "deserter" is really one of the greatest deserters of all time, having deserted many missing men it sent into the Vietnam quagmire.

Even if only one POW remains held against his will — either in Southeast Asia or in the Soviet Union where solid evidence indicates some were taken — then no resources of the U.S. government should be spared to locate him, get him out, and bring him home.

The shameful way this whole matter has been handled parallels the shameful way men were sent to Vietnam to fight with no intention of allowing them to win. Even though armed services personnel are told that our government has done everything possible on behalf of those left behind, the evidence continues to show that men were abandoned. The effect on the morale of our armed forces has been significant. One can only conclude that this and other devastating consequences were planned from the beginning.

Chapter 13

Get US out! of the United Nations

The Security Council thinks they are establishing a precedent.... Some of my colleagues think what they're trying to establish is a world government under which the Security Council is a council of Yodas. But they're not Yodas. And I'm not sure all of us would want to live under a government run by the politicians in the Security Council.

— Professor Alfred Rubin, Tufts University[1]

America's leaders are moving this nation inexorably toward complete submission to the United Nations. Step by step, and inch by inch, elected and appointed officials are eating away at national sovereignty, transferring control of our armed forces to the UN, and delivering the freedom of the American people to an emerging world government that will be led by internationalists who have no loyalty to any nation.

The steady progression of pro-UN and anti-American moves includes:

- U.S. troops are regularly being assigned to carry out UN missions.
- UN-empowering "disarmament" plans proceed toward completion.
- Successive Presidents have worked to establish suicidal pro-UN precedents.
- American taxpayers are forced to remain the largest "contributors" financing UN operations.
- The President has thrown a cloak of secrecy over extraordinary policy directives such as the UN-enhancing PDD-25.

• Our nation's military is being emasculated by allowing homosexuals to serve and by placing women in combat.

• The mission of our armed forces is being transformed from defending the United States to performing as the UN's policemen anywhere on earth.

• The U.S. Constitution, to which all perpetrators of these deeds have sworn a solemn oath, is ignored, circumvented, abrogated and overruled.

• The UN Secretary-General's plan to build a permanent UN Peace Force, which should be firmly opposed, enjoys favor within the highest levels of the U.S. government.

It is all there — and more. *If the perpetrators of this treachery are not exposed and derailed, Americans will soon see the end of this nation's independence and the destruction of their individual freedom.*

What will it mean for Americans if the world government zealots reach their goal? Tufts University Professor Alfred Rubin says his academic colleagues think the UN is "trying to establish a world government." He says his confreres have doubts about wanting "to live under a government run by politicians in the Security Council." These individuals are on the right track but mere doubts about a world government are not sufficient. There is an absolute need for massive opposition to such an effort.

There is probably nothing more misleading and infuriating than the insistent claim that the UN is a peace organization. It is not. It is a war organization that will, whenever given the opportunity, destroy whatever stands in the way of creating a "new world order" (socialism and world government). History shows that the UN will create war, prolong war, and even incite individuals to start war in order to achieve its goals.

But to answer the main question — what would life be like under a UN world government? — we turn back the pages of history to 1960 and to what happened in a place called Katanga.

Katanga Only Wanted Freedom

Prior to the 1950s and 1960s, European nations had colonized and civilized numerous parts of Africa. But beginning in those years, all of them either willingly abandoned or were unwillingly pressured out of their respective territories by contrived world opinion. New nations were being formed almost every month from domains that had previously been administered — or, in some cases, absorbed totally — by France, Belgium, England, Portugal, or the Netherlands. Practically all of these new nations were led from the outset by Soviet-trained native communists who established one-party dictatorships.

Belgium granted independence to its former Belgian Congo colony on June 30, 1960. Predictably, a Moscow-trained communist named Patrice Lumumba was "elected" to lead the nation. A vicious ex-convict, murderer, alcoholic, and drug addict, Lumumba unleashed an immediate reign of terror on the population. But not everyone was willing to capitulate and take the chance that things would work out beneficially.

Katanga, a province of this fledgling nation, had the good fortune to be led by a legitimately elected pro-Western, pro-free enterprise, and anti-communist native named Moise Tshombe, who had no intention of seeing his people and his province fall victim to the communist-led Congolese central government. So he did what dozens of other African leaders had done during this period: He declared independence for Katanga, stating, "I am seceding from chaos."

The United Nations, however, had others ideas. If Tshombe had been a communist, or even a pro-communist, the UN would have applauded his move just as it had done, and would continue to do, for the worst of Africa's new national leaders. The UN might even have welcomed him at UN headquarters in New York as it did Lumumba. Or a President of the United States might have warmly greeted Tshombe and had him stay overnight in the official presidential guest quarters as President Eisenhower had done in the case of Lumumba.

But Tshombe had not been trained in Moscow or Prague, had not imported Soviet and Czech "technicians," had not been equipped with Soviet arms, and was not a criminal. The UN would not allow him to establish an island of sanity in a continent becoming dominated by psychopathic communists and pro-communists.

For the next two years, the UN unleashed military fury on Katanga. Troops from Ireland, Sweden, Italy, Ethiopia, and India arrived in the province to wage war against a people whose only "crime" was their desire to avoid communist-inspired chaos and communist domination. UN forces were transported to do their dirty work by U.S. Air Force transports assigned by our government to enforce a UN resolution authorizing the use of military force against what were called "breakaway rebels" in Katanga.

Katanga was initially beaten down. After managing to recover for a while, the fledgling republic was beaten down for good. The UN did the beating.

During the UN-created carnage and terror, eyewitnesses reported that UN forces bombed hospitals, schools, and churches; machine-gunned and bayoneted women and children; and incarcerated tens of thousands of blacks in incredibly foul concentration camps. The "peace" organization systematically leveled much of the area.

Katanga enjoyed the benefit of a thriving medical community built by physicians from Belgium, Switzerland, Brazil, Spain, and Hungary.* In the midst of widespread terror and destruction courtesy of the UN, these doctors hastily compiled a report complete with photos detailing the atrocities and their source. Those who have seen a copy of *46 Angry Men* will have an answer to the question of what the world will be like should the UN take over completely.[2]

By the time the UN had finished several years of enforcing its

* Dr. Szeles, the chief doctor at the Prince Leopold Hospital in Elizabethville, had fled with his family from their native Hungary in 1948 when communists took control of that nation. Arriving in Katanga at the age of 50, he succeeded in building a new and productive life. But, he saw his home destroyed, his wife seriously wounded, and his hospital full of patients bombed on two occasions by the organization he was told had been created to save the world "from the scourge of war."

brand of "peace," Katanga's main cities lay in ruins and Moise Tshombe had been kidnapped never to be seen again. The most productive region of the former Belgian colony possessed tremendous mineral wealth and could once boast of a rising standard of living under its just and benevolent leaders. But the UN saw to it that its productivity was destroyed, its people brutalized, and its leader removed.[3]

Early in the war against Katanga, Patrice Lumumba was murdered as a result of a power struggle among his followers. Soviet dictator Nikita Khrushchev honored his memory in typical communist fashion by changing the name of Peoples Friendship University near Moscow to Patrice Lumumba Friendship University. And, with the UN's blessing, the group of thugs who had surrounded Lumumba chose another communist named Egide Bochely-Davidson to be Tshombe's replacement.[4] In keeping with its policy of helping communists and terrorists in every way possible, the UN actually transported Bochely-Davidson to Katanga's airport in one of its own planes. And the deputy UN civilian commander assigned to Katanga, who welcomed this communist on his arrival, was France's Michel Tombelaine, another communist.[5]

The final outcome of this treachery saw Katanga completely absorbed by the central government in what is now known as Zaire. The country has been led in recent decades by a thieving socialist named Mobutu Sese Seko who lives in splendor courtesy of loans from the UN-related World Bank and IMF. The people throughout Zaire, however, are among the poorest in the entire world.

It cannot be stated too often or too loudly: The fledgling nation of Katanga was targeted and destroyed by the UN because its people rejected communism and wanted to be free. The "peace" organization never targeted Soviet-backed dictatorships, only those lands where communism and submission to the planned new world order were not welcomed. Katanga was first, but Rhodesia, Southwest Africa, and other nations would feel the sting of the UN in the years ahead.

If the UN is given sufficient power, the fate of Katanga will descend on any nation or even any portion of a nation that resists the designs of the world organization and its promoters. And, if the American people do not stop the steady transfer of our nation's military to the UN, American troops in the UN's blue helmets will enforce the UN's will throughout the world while troops from elsewhere will arrive in a defenseless America to establish UN rule here.

The Barbarism of UN Troops

In their justifiably angry report about UN atrocities in Katanga, the 46 civilian doctors denounced the "savage U.N.O. Indian troops" who had bombarded "hospitals, missions, churches, and civilian habitations." They condemned the "Ethiopians who fire at sight on anyone and anything"; the "odious crimes of the Gurkha mercenaries of the U.N.O."; the Swedish mercenaries whose "armed arrests and brutalities" constituted "a slavish imitation of the methods worthy of the Gestapo"; and "the Swedish and Irish mercenaries of the U.N.O." who shelled a hospital filled with 700 patients.

In one of their 30 desperate telegrams sent to world leaders, the doctors accused UN mercenaries from Ethiopia of "assassinations of peaceful civilians, numerous rape cases, looting, and robbery with violence." This same message stated, "It would be sufficient to search Ethiopian baggage to recover wedding rings, money, and precious objects stolen by mercenaries."

The barbarism witnessed in Katanga has never been punished. It is, therefore, reasonable to assume that it was countenanced and will be repeated. Men who are thrown into a multi-national force in some faraway land have little reason to restrain their passions and will submit to their worst inclinations, especially if such conduct is tolerated or encouraged by UN leaders. Even CFR member Charles Krauthammer stated in a 1993 *Time* magazine column that the UN's "soldiers wear the same colored hats, but they have differently colored allegiances."[6] And we might add, they also have different colored morals.

In November 1994, newspapers throughout Canada published grizzly photos of a dead Somali teenager who had been tortured and beaten to death by Canadian UN troops.[7] The *Toronto Star*, Canada's most widely circulated newspaper, showed one of the photos under the headline, "Canada's Shame."

In February 1994, a UN official in Mozambique admitted that some UN troops deployed in that country had engaged in sexual activity with children and had boosted the prostitution industry enormously.[8]

As an indication of the priorities set by the UN, the January 25, 1993 issue of the Stockholm, Sweden publication *Aftonbladet* reported: "A half million condoms, large and small, have been sent to Cambodia in order to make happy the 15,700 UN soldiers who shall shape the peace there, it has been reported from Phnom Penh."

In 1988, Jozef Verbeek, the director of the UNICEF Committee in Belgium, and UNICEF employee Michel Felu were convicted of child pornography and child prostitution by a Brussels court. Police had discovered that a pornography ring of which they were a part had been secretly using a room in the basement of the UNICEF headquarters where their activity had been centered. Police seized 19,000 pornographic photos of children, many of whom were under ten years of age. Police discovery of a UNICEF computer that contained a mailing list of over 400 names in 15 European nations led to additional arrests in several other European nations.[9]

In 1975, Congressman Larry McDonald (D-GA) reported that UNICEF had supplied "$40.2 million to communist regimes in Indochina with no strings attached." He stated: "While America was donating $45.8 million to UNICEF — including $6.1 million collected by trick-or-treating youngsters ... the funds were converted into medical supplies, trucks and equipment used in the takeover of our ally, the Republic of South Vietnam."[10]

In September 1964, the Greek Cypriot government arrested five Swedish members of the UN peacekeeping force in Cyprus and charged them with smuggling guns to Turkish Cypriots.[11]

During the 1980s, Lebanon became famous for terrorist activity. More than 200 U.S. Marines were killed in a single terrorist bombing attack while serving in a compound at the Beirut airport. Much of the various types of terrorism in Lebanon was known to have originated in Syria. Several American hostages had been captured, one of whom was CIA operative William Buckley. While searching for Buckley in Lebanon, U.S. Navy officer Michael J. Walsh found himself confronted by UN personnel. A member of the legendary Navy SEALs (the elite SEa, Air, and Land force), Walsh included the following passage in a book about his many experiences:

> While I was there, a small group of U.N. soldiers arrived, the usual hodgepodge of international military heroes. They asked what we were doing, being very polite, as my escort and I were in civilian clothes. For a moment I was whisked aside by Buckley's man and advised to be careful what I told the U.N. guys, some of whom were known to be passing information on U.S. forces directly to the Syrians.[12]

What, after all, can be expected from UN troops when the organization's leadership countenances the worst kind of treachery and immorality? In January 1994, the U.S. State Department and the U.S. Senate protested the UN's official ties to the North American Man-Boy Love Association (NAMBLA), a group supporting pedophilia.[13] Can there be a lower form of humanity? Yet NAMBLA has been accorded official status by the UN.

UN Creates War in Somalia

While the conduct of UN troops is frequently deplorable and even barbaric, the UN's penchant for stimulating military action and creating war for its own purposes is an even greater crime. In his July 26, 1993 *Time* magazine commentary, Charles Krauthammer, a supporter of the UN, wrote the following about the American-led UN operation in Somalia:

> We waded ashore in Somalia to feed the hungry. Now our gunships hover over Mogadishu shooting rockets into crowded villas.

> Blue-helmeted U.N. troops, once a symbol of ineffectiveness but at least innocuousness, now fire into a crowd of demonstrators. At least 20 women and children die. The Security Council stoutly defends the massacre.[14]

It was President George Bush who had so dramatically boosted the image of the UN with his completely unconstitutional war against Saddam Hussein. Later, it was the same George Bush who, on December 4, 1992, sent 30,000 U.S. troops to Somalia in a UN mission whose purpose he said was "to ease suffering and save lives ... to ensure the safe delivery of the food the Somalis need to survive." He emphasized: "This operation is not open-ended." But, as the UN has demonstrated and Mr. Bush surely knew, there is no such thing as a UN mission that is not open-ended.

In no time at all in Somalia, our nation's troops and those of other nations were ordered to disarm competing militia, capture Somali criminals, create police and judicial systems, and rebuild Somalia's infrastructure. When the UN decided to apprehend "warlord" Mohamed Aidid, the mission escalated to an unvarnished military operation. Early in August 1993, the Italian general commanding his nation's 2,600-man contingent pulled all of his troops out of Mogadishu and refused to follow orders from UN superiors. Brigadier General Bruno Loi steadfastly maintained that the Somali relief effort "started out as a humanitarian mission [and] it must remain a humanitarian mission."[15]

But the American forces were not fortunate enough to be serving under a commander like Italy's General Loi. On October 3, 1993, U.S. Army Rangers were ordered to capture Aidid but ran into a force of armed Somalis. The operation resulted in 18 dead Americans and 75 wounded. Television news programs throughout the U.S. showed horrifying footage of the body of an American soldier being dragged through the streets by angry Somalis. (An inquiry into this disaster concluded in May 1994 that the Rangers' request for more air power had been denied by senior officials; the raid was characterized by the media as "botched.")[16]

The humanitarians in charge of this UN operation had chosen sides in the Somali versus Somali struggle. Aidid had been declared the "bad guy," and the "peacekeepers" were now combatants. Men on both sides died in several skirmishes. The UN had started a war, and some of its adherents were delighted. At the UN, Secretary-General Boutros Boutros-Ghali proclaimed that the UN's mission had been expanded. A headline in the *Washington Post* for October 9th said it all: "Boutros-Ghali Sees Somalia as Key To Establishing New Role For U.N."[17] That new role certainly appears to be military enforcement of the UN's will.

Report Shows UN Was the Aggressor

The UN claims that its humanitarian effort in Somalia was converted to a military operation because 24 Pakistani UN soldiers had been killed by Somalis on June 5, 1993. In the wake of that incident, the Security Council declared on June 7th that it was "gravely alarmed at the premeditated attack" and formally authorized the Secretary-General "to take all necessary measures against those responsible." The humanitarians were now pressed into the role of combatants.

The UN turned to Professor Tom Farer of Washington DC's American University to investigate the incident and to justify its dramatic and costly upgrading of its presence in Somalia. Farer, a member of the CFR, sought to do so and, after he completed his work on August 23, 1993, the UN issued a self-serving summary of his report. The full report had been declared secret by the UN and requests from the public, the press, and U.S. officials for a copy were rebuffed. But Tom Wigod, a determined California investigator, spent months of effort and finally acquired the 109-page Farer Report out of the UN.[18]

While dispensing copies of the report and relying on the information it supplies, Wigod showed that the UN's seizure of Radio Mogadishu was the provocation leading to the June 5th bloody clash. That radio station was the area's only broadcast medium and the major source for news of any kind for the entire area. It was deemed essential by many, certainly including Aidid and his people. Defending it from the UN's obvious intention to shut it down made sense to Aidid.

With the Farer Report showing the fraudulence of the UN's claim that the attack on its forces was "premeditated," it is small wonder that the UN tried to keep it secret.

The Farer report also supplied abundant evidence that Aidid had cautioned his followers not to attack UN troops and that the attack launched by his men on UN troops was a spontaneous response to the attempted seizure of the radio station.

The bottom line here, as the Farer Report's evidence shows, is that the UN created a serious provocation and then built on it as part of a continuing drive to acquire more power. The UN, which desperately wants a full-time "peace force" and wants U.S. troops to do its dirty work, hired a friend to investigate its misdeeds and then tried to hide his UN-indicting report when it told some truth.

Earlier, we stated that the UN will start a war to serve its own purposes. This is precisely what occurred in Somalia and in Katanga. The purpose was to convince the world that it must have that full-time "peace force." If Pakistanis, Americans, Italians, and Somalis have to die along the way, that's okay. Empowering the UN by any means, fair or foul, is the goal. The world organization will seize upon any incident, even create one where none exists, to further its global designs.

The thought of a UN in possession of an all-powerful UN Army is a nightmare that must never be allowed to become real. The passions of immoral and ambitious men have to be restrained by government, not given free rein. Yet, the UN Charter contains none of the restraints that can be found in the U.S. Constitution.

Good government is always an impediment to tyrants. The American people are being led to give up the American system, with its checks and balances, diffusion of powers, and separation of powers, and replace it with a UN system that is a blueprint for tyranny. And most Americans have no awareness about any part of what is truly happening right before their eyes.

The Founding Fathers of our nation would be aghast to know that anyone in America would favor the UN. They expected that our nation would continue to be filled with moral and informed citizens who understood the principles undergirding liberty and justice and who would ever be on guard to defend them.

Stop the UN Before It's Too Late

If United States support for the UN can be removed, the organization will fade away and die as did its predecessor, the League of Nations. Other nations will follow the U.S. lead as many have often done in the past.

Without U.S. military might under its control, the UN will never possess its all-powerful "UN Peace Force."

If our nation terminates the steady transfer of our armed forces to UN control and removes our military from all entangling UN-related commitments, the world organization will be stymied. It will not be able to use U.S. forces to compel the peoples of the world to submit to its will, and it will not be able to employ foreign troops to do likewise to Americans.

If enough people in this nation can be given the full truth about the UN and its many high-level promoters — instead of the constant stream of pro-UN propaganda — the people of this nation will see to it that their representatives in Congress take action to *Get US out!*

George Washington once stated that "truth will ultimately prevail where there is pains taken to bring it to light." Pains must be taken by many more Americans if this nation is to remain free. Will you help?

One of Daniel Webster's most frequently quoted statements is, "There is nothing so powerful as truth, and often nothing so strange." It may seem strange but it is true that the "peace" organization is a war organization, that its vaunted claim to be a fountain of justice in a mean and vindictive world is a hoax, and that its protestations of protecting human rights and enhancing human freedoms are demonstrable lies.

It is also true that the greatest promoters of UN world domination and the most important enemies of U.S. sovereignty serve in leadership posts in this nation. The UN could not survive for long without support from top officials of this nation. These personages intend to have the UN — which they will control — rule the world. And they will countenance treason, lying, killing, and any other foul means imaginable to accomplish their goal.

Borrowing the words of the Lord Himself, we say to fellow Americans, "And you shall know the truth, and the truth shall make you free." What we have presented in these pages is truth that must be disseminated widely and acted upon as if one's life depended upon doing so — because it does!

If enough truth reaches enough Americans, they will choose new leaders who will withdraw this nation from the UN, rebuild our armed forces, and ensure that our military serves nothing but this nation. If enough good people decide to join the ever-growing army of patriotic Americans dedicated to exposing and routing the conspiracy in our midst, then America will remain a bastion of freedom for ourselves and for the children of today and tomorrow.

How about you? Your help is needed — and needed now. Will you give it? Our recommendation to all is simple: Contact The John Birch Society and get started in the vitally important work of saving this nation from a United Nations type of world.

Appendix A

What is the Council on Foreign Relations?

There exists in our nation today a privately run organization with only 3,000 members, several hundred of whom are U.S. government officials. But even though this organization possesses enormous influence over the actions of our national government, most Americans have never heard of it.

This same organization's members dominate our nation's mass media, multinational corporations, the banking industry, colleges and universities, even the military. Yet its domination is unknown to the average citizen.

The members of this small but extremely influential group are responsible for a parade of foreign policy disasters in China, Korea, Vietnam, Nicaragua, Panama, Cuba, and Africa. The group itself has always sought to lead the United States into a one-world socialistic system led by its members and their like-minded associates in other nations.

Shouldn't you know about this organization and what its members are planning for the 1990s?

This appendix will introduce you to the Council on Foreign Relations, the little-known New York City-based organization that is both the seat of the liberal Establishment and the main force pushing the United States into the new world order.

CFR Wants One-World Socialism

It was a disappointed but determined group of diplomats from the United States and England who gathered at the Majestic Hotel in Paris on June 17, 1919. Their disappointment stemmed from the U.S. Senate's rejection of America's proposed entry into world government via the League of Nations. But they remained determined to scrap the sovereignty of each of their nations, and all nations.

The leader of the U.S. contingent at this 1919 conference was President Woodrow Wilson's top advisor, Edward Mandell House. In his 1912 book, *Philip Dru: Administrator*, House laid out a plan for radically altering the American system via what he termed a "conspiracy." The book supplied his ultimate goal: "Socialism as dreamed of by Karl Marx."

The Paris gathering led to the formation of the British Royal Institute for International Affairs and the American Council on Foreign Relations (CFR). With Rockefeller and Carnegie money backing it, the CFR quickly attracted influential Americans who used their influence to labor for the one-world socialist goal. In 1939, the organization accepted a formal invitation to establish a relationship with the U.S. State Department. That relationship soon grew into CFR domination of the foreign policy of our nation. Practically every Secretary of State for the past 50 years — serving both Democratic and Republican Administrations — has held CFR membership.

Explicitly Stated Goal

As early as 1922, the CFR's prestigious journal, *Foreign Affairs*, brazenly called for "world government" at the expense of our nation's independence. Repeatedly airing this subversive goal over subsequent years, *Foreign Affairs* published its most explicit call for the termination of U.S. sovereignty in Richard N. Gardner's 1974 article entitled "The Hard Road to World Order."

Admitting that "instant world government" was unfortunately unattainable, the Columbia University professor and former State Department official proceeded to champion "an end run around national sovereignty, eroding it piece by piece." He also pointed to numerous international groups and causes, each of which he claimed "can produce some remarkable concessions of sovereignty that could not be achieved on an across-the-board basis."

At the time this article appeared, hundreds of CFR members were holding high government posts. Those who were required to swear an oath to support the Constitution of the United States should have immediately resigned from the CFR. None did. Nor were any asked to do so by superiors in government. Instead, the erosion of national independence and the undermining of the Constitution continued.

CFR members like Gardner have historically helped similarly determined world-government advocates achieve power in other nations. It didn't matter to them whether foreign leaders were professed socialists, communists, or whatever, as long as they shared Edward Mandell House's goal of "Socialism as dreamed of by Karl Marx." Marxism was the goal, and that has always meant economic control of the people *and* world government.

Over the years, therefore, CFR members have carried out the Marxist goals of their organization's founder when they helped one communist thug after another take control of once-free nations. Now that communism is no longer the favored route to socialist world government, CFR members have thrown the weight of their considerable influence behind socialists and "former" communists in Europe, Africa, and elsewhere. But they deserve condemnation for the deaths of hundreds of millions killed by communist rulers, and for the horror of life under communist dictatorships still endured by more than a billion human beings.

Past Treachery

CFR members Owen Lattimore and Dean Acheson engineered the betrayal of Chiang Kai-Shek's government and the domination of the Chinese people by the bloodiest murderers the world has ever known.

CFR members Dean Acheson and Dean Rusk arranged for the no-win undeclared war in Korea, the removal from command of General MacArthur who sought victory, and the establishment of Communist Red China as the primary military power in Asia.

CFR members John Foster Dulles and Allen Dulles, filling top posts in the Administration of CFR member Dwight Eisenhower, betrayed the Hungarian Freedom Fighters in 1956 and knowingly aided communist Fidel Castro in his successful seizure of Cuba in 1958-59.

CFR members McGeorge Bundy, Adlai Stevenson, and John J. McCloy saw to it that the 1961 Bay of Pigs invasion was a miserable failure, a huge boost for Castro, and a stunning embarrassment for the United States.

CFR members Dean Rusk, Robert McNamara, and Henry Cabot Lodge pushed the United States into Vietnam and drew up the rules of engagement for our forces that made victory completely unattainable. CFR members Richard Nixon and Henry Kissinger continued those policies, presided over America's total defeat in 1973, and allowed South Vietnam, Laos, and Cambodia to be delivered to communist rulers.

CFR stalwarts Henry Kissinger, Ellsworth Bunker, and Sol Linowitz arranged (with Senate approval) in 1978 to give away the U.S. canal in Panama to a Marxist dictatorship and to sweeten the incredible deal with a gift of $400 million to take it.

CFR leaders Zbigniew Brzezinski, Cyrus Vance, and Warren Christopher undermined strong U.S. allies in Nicaragua and Iran during the 1970s and helped anti-American and Marxist leaders to power.

CFR members George Shultz, William J. Casey, and Malcolm Baldrige, during the 1980s, continued the policy of supplying U.S. aid which kept communists in power in Poland, Romania, China, and the Soviet Union. These same individuals did all they could to assist and dignify the Marxists in El Salvador, Nicaragua, and South Africa. Wherever communist regimes failed, they sent more U.S. aid to the socialists and one-worlders who came to power.

CFR leaders in the Administration of CFR veteran George Bush continued to undermine the government of South Africa until it fell into the hands of Marxist Nelson Mandela.

CFR veteran George Bush deliberately avoided the U.S. Congress and went to the United Nations for authorization to unleash American military forces against Iraq in 1991. He pointedly stated that his goal was a "new world order ... a United Nations that performs as envisioned by its founders." The UN's founders, however, included 43 current or future members of the CFR. A leader of the U.S. delegation and the Secretary-General of the UN's founding conference in 1945 was future CFR member and secret communist Alger Hiss.

CFR member Bill Clinton has followed the Marxist game plan called for by Edward Mandell House by crusading for socialized medicine, an end to private ownership of firearms, and creating economic unions preceding world government through NAFTA and GATT. President Clinton has also embarked on a deliberate program, most notably via his April 1994 Presidential Decision Directive 25, which urges turning over control of U.S. military forces to the United Nations.

Destroying Checks and Balances

Americans have always been assured that tyranny cannot be established in our nation because of our Constitution's brilliant system of checks and balances. In a round-robin way, each of the three branches of government has the power to check and limit the activities of the other two. This feature of the Constitution did not materialize by chance. In *The Federalist Papers*, James Madison wrote: "The accumulation of all powers, legislative, executive and judiciary, in the same hand, whether of one, a few, or many, or whether hereditary, self-appointed or elected, may justly be pronounced the very definition of tyranny." But through its members, the CFR is amassing exactly the kind of tyrannical power Madison feared.

The Executive Branch is led by CFR member Bill Clinton. His top appointees include CFR members Madeleine Albright, Bruce Babbitt, Lloyd Bentsen (former CFR), Warren Christopher, Henry Cisneros, W. Anthony Lake, Alice Rivlin, Donna Shalala, Strobe Talbott, R. James Woolsey, and a host of others.

Thirteen of the 100 seats in the Legislative Branch's Senate are filled by CFR members John Chafee, William Cohen, Christopher Dodd, Bob Graham, John Kerry, Joseph Lieberman, Patrick Moynihan, Claiborne Pell, Larry Pressler, Charles Robb, John D.

Rockefeller IV, William Roth, and Olympia Snowe. The most important officer of the House of Representatives, Speaker Newt Gingrich, is a CFR member. In addition, there are eleven other members of the CFR serving in the House.

The Judicial Branch consists of the Supreme Court and all federal district and appeals courts. Of the nine justices of the nation's highest court, three are CFR members: Sandra Day O'Connor, Ruth Bader Ginsburg, and Stephen G. Breyer.

Checks and balances? The CFR doesn't worry about them at all. But every American should carefully consider James Madison's warning.

Grip on the Mass Media

Why are Americans unaware of the enormous clout possessed by the CFR? How can it be that an organization formed to undo the American dream and lead this nation into a one-world Marxist nightmare can achieve such a controlling influence without the people knowing about it? Why hasn't the supposedly tough and courageous mass media informed the people about this subversive takeover?

The answer, very simply, is that the CFR dominates the mass media, which only rarely reports anything about the organization. The names of hundreds of media executives and journalists can be found on the CFR membership roster. On October 30, 1993, *Washington Post* columnist Richard Harwood detailed the CFR's domination of his own profession in his column entitled "Ruling Class Journalists." While never condemning what he was reporting, and likely steering ambitious individuals toward the Council, Harwood characterized CFR members as "the nearest thing we have to a ruling establishment in the United States." He wrote:

> In the past 15 years, council directors have included Hedley Donovan of Time Inc., Elizabeth Drew of the New Yorker, Philip Geyelin of The Washington Post, Karen Elliott House of the Wall Street Journal, and Strobe Talbott of Time magazine, who is now President Clinton's [Deputy Secretary of State]. The editorial page

editor, deputy editorial page editor, executive editor, managing editor, foreign editor, national affairs editor, business and financial editor and various writers as well as Katharine Graham, the paper's principal owner, represent *The Washington Post* in the council's membership. The executive editor, managing editor and foreign editor of the *New York Times* are members, along with the executives of such other large newspapers as the *Wall Street Journal* and *Los Angeles Times*, the weekly news magazines, network television executives and celebrities — Dan Rather, Tom Brokaw and Jim Lehrer, for example — and various columnists, among them Charles Krauthammer, William F. Buckley, George Will and Jim Hoagland.

Americans who wish to be well informed must seek better sources and sounder perspective such as can be found in *The New American* magazine. Relying on popular newspapers, magazines, and radio/television networks is asking to be programed by the Establishment.

Secret Modus Operandi

The Council repeatedly denies that it sets policy for our nation. Yet, while discussing our nation's changing foreign policy, CFR chairman Peter G. Peterson stated in the organization's 1989 *Annual Report* that "the Board of Directors and the staff of the Council have decided that this institution should play a leadership role in defining these new foreign policy agenda."

Our question is simply: How can an organization define an agenda for the nation without taking a stand or advocating a policy? The answer is that it can't. Any claim from the CFR that it is merely a debating forum open to all ideas is absurd. Even Richard Harwood knows this. In his *Washington Post* article mentioned previously, he wrote that the CFR journalists he listed "do not merely analyze and interpret foreign policy; they help make it."

The actual content of meetings held at the group's headquarters and elsewhere remains a closely guarded secret. According to CFR bylaws, it is an "express condition of membership" that members refrain from disclosing in any way what goes on at Council meetings. Any action contravening this rule "may be regarded by the Board of Directors in its sole discretion as ground for termination or suspension of membership."

Yet, cabinet officials, members of Congress, high-ranking military officers, and other government officials repeatedly participate at CFR functions. Such "confidential" gatherings under the aegis of a private organization (especially one founded by an individual whose goal was "Socialism as dreamed of by Karl Marx") are totally inconsistent with proper conduct in a free country.

No CFR member is ever directly instructed to hold any particular view. Instead, government officials and media personalities supply important respectability for favored positions, and render varying degrees of disdain or contempt for the opposite view. Ambitious politicians, journalists, corporate executives, professors, and others dutifully follow the lead set for them — frequently without ever knowing whose attitude they are parroting. In this way, an agenda is indeed set and policies are established.

As a rule, slight variations on most topics are tolerated, even welcomed. But advocacy of any position outside carefully drawn limits earns scorn and ridicule. For example, discussion about increasing or decreasing U.S. funding for either the United Nations or a variety of foreign aid projects is tolerated, even welcomed. But anyone who calls for U.S. withdrawal from the world body, or who recommends that all foreign aid be terminated, jeopardizes his or her reputation with the nation's most prestigious power brokers.

Those who read CFR publications and study the editorial stance of CFR-controlled media organs know exactly which are the favored attitudes. The CFR and several like-minded groups can be expected to support the following: more pacts, treaties, and agreements that compromise U.S. sovereignty; continued praise for and reliance on the United Nations; piecemeal transfer of U.S. military forces to UN supervision and command; more and newer forms of foreign aid; undermining and isolation of any national leader who does not favor socialism and world government under a "new world order"; and submission to the radical demands of environmental extremists, population planners, and human rights crusaders who will never be satisfied until the United States no longer exists as a free and independent nation.

Some who follow the lead of the Establishment are undoubtedly committed to the world government and socialism advocated by Marx and the CFR's founders. But most who toe this line are self-promoters who are interested only in re-election, advancement, and recognition. They care little or nothing about the Constitution, their fellow citizens, and freedom in general.

The Shadows of Power

A thoroughly revealing history of the Council on Foreign Relations and its responsibility for America's decline is available in researcher James Perloff's superb book, *The Shadows of Power*. Unlike others who have sought to warn the American people about the pervasive power of the CFR, Mr. Perloff studied the organization's publications from its inception in 1921. The evidence he supplies to support his condemnation is taken from the CFR itself. His important book concludes that the CFR is a major participant in an ongoing conspiratorial drive to use the U.S. government and the wealth of the American people to create power over mankind for a few diabolically driven individuals.

Mr. Perloff is careful to point out that only some of the CFR's members are completely committed to the sinister goals he exposes. He believes, as does The John Birch Society, that many CFR members, and many others who follow the group's lead, would readily switch their allegiance should widespread awareness be created about this powerful organization's history and designs.

You can help to terminate CFR domination of our nation's affairs by reading and distributing *The Shadows of Power*. You can also participate in a nationwide effort to preserve freedom for the American people and independence for our nation by participating in the programs of The John Birch Society. Unless many more Americans become better informed and begin to take an active role in shaping our nation's affairs, the freedoms we have all taken for granted will disappear and the darkness of brutal totalitarianism will descend upon us. None of us want an all-powerful tyrannical government dictating to each of us how we may live, what we may say, and whom we must serve. But all of that is surely on the horizon unless proper action is taken soon.

The John Birch Society

Founded in December 1958 by a group led by Robert Welch, the John Birch Society is named for Captain John Birch, the remarkable missionary-turned-soldier who served with exemplary valor during World War II and was brutally murdered by Chinese communists in 1945.

The Society has always sought to create awareness about the marvelous system of government given us by America's founders *and* about the forces seeking to destroy it. Never a "political" organization backing candidates, the organization believes that an educated electorate is the key to victory. Its overall goals appear in the motto, "Less government, more responsibility, and — with God's help — a better world." Membership is open to men and women of good character and noble ideals from all races, ethnic backgrounds, and religions. You are cordially invited to investigate its work.

This appendix is adapted from an article which originally appeared in September 1994 under the title "Americans Have a Right to Know About the Council on Foreign Relations."

FREEDOM FROM WAR

THE UNITED STATES PROGRAM FOR GENERAL AND COMPLETE DISARMAMENT IN A PEACEFUL WORLD

The following is the complete, verbatim text of the September 1961 State Department Document Freedom From War: The United States Program for General and Complete Disarmament in a Peaceful World *(also known as "Department of State Publication 7277"). Although the implications of this treasonous document are discussed in chapter 10, we are providing the full text here so that you can read it and judge for yourself its sovereigny-destroying provisions.*

Introduction

The revolutionary development of modern weapons within a world divided by serious ideological differences has produced a crisis in human history. In order to overcome the danger of nuclear war now confronting mankind, the United States has introduced at the Sixteenth General Assembly of the United Nations a *Program for General and Complete Disarmament in a Peaceful World.*

This new program provides for the progressive reduction of the war-making capabilities of nations and the simultaneous strengthening of international institutions to settle disputes and maintain the peace. It sets forth a series of comprehensive measures which can and should be taken in order to bring about a world in which there will be freedom from war and security for all states. It is based on three principles deemed essential to the achievement of practical progress in the disarmament field:

First, there must be immediate disarmament action:

A strenuous and uninterrupted effort must be made toward the goal of general and complete disarmament; at the same time, it is important that specific measures be put into effect as soon as possible.

Second, all disarmament obligations must be subject to effective international controls:

The control organization must have the manpower, facilities, and effectiveness to assure that limitations or reductions take place as agreed. It must also be able to certify to all states that retained forces and armaments do not exceed those permitted at any stage of the disarmament process.

Third, adequate peace-keeping machinery must be established: There is an inseparable relationship between the scaling down of national armaments on the one hand and the building up of international peace-keeping machinery and institutions on the other. Nations are unlikely to shed their means of self-protection in the absence of alternative ways to safeguard their legitimate interests. This can only be achieved through the progressive strengthening of international institutions under the United Nations and by creating a United Nations Peace Force to enforce the peace as the disarmament process proceeds.

There follows a summary of the principal provisions of the United States *Program for General and Complete Disarmament in a Peaceful World*. The full text of the program is contained in an appendix to this pamphlet.

FREEDOM FROM WAR

THE UNITED STATES PROGRAM FOR GENERAL AND COMPLETE DISARMAMENT IN A PEACEFUL WORLD

Summary

DISARMAMENT GOAL AND OBJECTIVES

The over-all goal of the United States is a free, secure, and peaceful world of independent states adhering to common standards of justice and international conduct and subjecting the use of force to the rule of law; a world which has achieved general and complete disarmament under effective international control; and a world in which adjustment to change takes place in accordance with the principles of the United Nations.

In order to make possible the achievement of that goal, the program sets forth the following specific objectives toward which nations should direct their efforts:

- The disbanding of all national armed forces and the prohibition of their reestablishment in any form whatsoever other than those required to preserve internal order and for contributions to a United Nations Peace Force;
- The elimination from national arsenals of all armaments, including all weapons of mass destruction and the means for their delivery, other

than those required for a United Nations Peace Force and for maintaining internal order;

- The institution of effective means for the enforcement of international agreements, for the settlement of disputes, and for the maintenance of peace in accordance with the principles of the United Nations;
- The establishment and effective operation of an International Disarmament Organization within the framework of the United Nations to insure compliance at all times with all disarmament obligations.

TASK OF NEGOTIATING STATES

The negotiating states are called upon to develop the program into a detailed plan for general and complete disarmament and to continue their efforts without interruption until the whole program has been achieved. To this end, they are to seek the widest possible area of agreement at the earliest possible date. At the same time, and without prejudice to progress on the disarmament program, they are to seek agreement on those immediate measures that would contribute to the common security of nations and that could facilitate and form part of the total program.

GOVERNING PRINCIPLES

The program sets forth a series of general principles to guide the negotiating states in their work. These make clear that:

- As states relinquish their arms, the United Nations must be progressively strengthened in order to improve its capacity to assure international security and the peaceful settlement of disputes;
- Disarmament must proceed as rapidly as possible, until it is completed, in stages containing balanced, phased, and safeguarded measures;
- Each measure and stage should be carried out in an agreed period of time, with transition from one stage to the next to take place as soon as all measures in the preceding stage have been carried out and verified and as soon as necessary arrangements for verification of the next stage have been made;
- Inspection and verification must establish both that nations carry out scheduled limitations or reductions and that they do not retain armed forces and armaments in excess of those permitted at any stage of the disarmament process; and
- Disarmament must take place in a manner that will not affect adversely the security of any state.

DISARMAMENT STAGES

The program provides for progressive disarmament steps to take place in three stages and for the simultaneous strengthening of international institutions.

FIRST STAGE

The first stage contains measures which would significantly reduce the capabilities of nations to wage aggressive war. Implementation of this stage would mean that:

- **The nuclear threat would be reduced:**

All states would have adhered to a treaty effectively prohibiting the testing of nuclear weapons.

The production of fissionable materials for use in weapons would be stopped and quantities of such materials from past production would be converted to non-weapons uses.

States owning nuclear weapons would not relinquish control of such weapons to any nation not owning them and would not transmit to any such nation information or material necessary for their manufacture.

States not owning nuclear weapons would not manufacture them or attempt to obtain control of such weapons belonging to other states.

A Commission of Experts would be established to report on the feasibility and means for the verified reduction and eventual elimination of nuclear weapons stockpiles.

- **Strategic delivery vehicles would be reduced:**

Strategic nuclear weapons delivery vehicles of specified categories and weapons designed to counter such vehicles would be reduced to agreed levels by equitable and balanced steps; their production would be discontinued or limited; their testing would be limited or halted.

- **Arms and armed forces would be reduced:**

The armed forces of the United States and the Soviet Union would be limited to 2.1 million men each (with appropriate levels not exceeding that amount for other militarily significant states); levels of armaments would be correspondingly reduced and their production would be limited.

An Experts Commission would be established to examine and report on the feasibility and means of accomplishing verifiable reduction and eventual elimination of all chemical, biological and radiological weapons.

- **Peaceful use of outer space would be promoted:**

The placing in orbit or stationing in outer space of weapons capable of producing mass destruction would be prohibited.

States would give advance notification of space vehicle and missile launchings.

- **U.N. peace-keeping powers would be strengthened:**

Measures would be taken to develop and strengthen United Nations arrangements for arbitration, for the development of international law, and for the establishment in Stage II of a permanent U.N. Peace Force.

- **An International Disarmament Organization would be established for effective verification of the disarmament program:**

Its functions would be expanded progressively as disarmament proceeds.

It would certify to all states that agreed reductions have taken place and that retained forces and armaments do not exceed permitted levels.

It would determine the transition from one stage to the next.

- **States would be committed to other measures to reduce international tension and to protect against the chance of war by accident, miscalculation, or surprise attack:**

States would be committed to refrain from the threat or use of any type of armed force contrary to the principles of the U.N. Charter and to refrain from indirect aggression and subversion against any country.

A U.N. peace observation group would be available to investigate any situation which might constitute a threat to or breach of the peace.

States would be committed to give advance notice of major military movements which might cause alarm; observation posts would be established to report on concentrations and movements of military forces.

SECOND STAGE

The second stage contains a series of measures which would bring within sight a world in which there would be freedom from war. Implementation of all measures in the second stage would mean:

- Further substantial reductions in the armed forces, armaments, and military establishments of states, including strategic nuclear weapons delivery vehicles and countering weapons;
- Further development of methods for the peaceful settlement of disputes under the United Nations:
- Establishment of a permanent international peace force within the United Nations;
- Depending on the findings of an Experts Commission, a halt in the production of chemical, bacteriological, and radiological weapons and a reduction of existing stocks or their conversion to peaceful uses;
- On the basis of the findings of an Experts Commission, a reduction of stocks of nuclear weapons;
- The dismantling or the conversion to peaceful uses of certain military bases and facilities wherever located; and
- The strengthening and enlargement of the International Disarmament Organization to enable it to verify the steps taken in Stage II and to determine the transition to Stage III.

THIRD STAGE

During the third stage of the program, the states of the world, building on the experience and confidence gained in successfully implementing the measures of the first two stages, would take final steps toward the goal of a world in which:

- States would retain only those forces, non-nuclear armaments, and establishments required for the purpose of maintaining internal order; they would also support and provide agreed manpower for a U.N. Peace Force.
- The U.N. Peace Force, equipped with agreed types and quantities of armaments, would be fully functioning.
- The manufacture of armaments would be prohibited except for those of agreed types and quantities to be used by the U.N. Peace Force and those required to maintain internal order. All other armaments would be destroyed or converted to peaceful purposes.
- The peace-keeping capabilities of the United Nations would be sufficiently strong and the obligations of all states under such arrangements sufficiently far-reaching as to assure peace and the just settlement of differences in a disarmed world.

Appendix

DECLARATION ON DISARMAMENT

THE UNITED STATES PROGRAM FOR GENERAL AND COMPLETE DISARMAMENT IN A PEACEFUL WORLD

The Nations of the world,

Conscious of the crisis in human history produced by the revolutionary development of modern weapons within a world divided by serious ideological differences;

Determined to save present and succeeding generations from the scourge of war and the dangers and burdens of the arms race and to create conditions in which all peoples can strive freely and peacefully to fulfill their basic aspirations;

Declare their goal to be: A free, secure, and peaceful world of independent states adhering to common standards of justice and international conduct and subjecting the use of force to the rule of law; a world where adjustment to change takes place in accordance with the principles of the United Nations; a world where there shall be a permanent state of general and complete disarmament under effective international control and where the resources of nations shall be devoted to man's material, cultural, and spiritual advance;

Set forth as the objectives of a program of general and complete disarmament in a peaceful world:

(a) The disbanding of all national armed forces and the prohibition of their reestablishment in any form whatsoever other than those required to preserve internal order and for contributions to a United Nations Peace Force;

(b) The elimination from national arsenals of all armaments, including all weapons of mass destruction and the means for their delivery, other than those required for a United Nations Peace Force and for maintaining internal order;

(c) The establishment and effective operation of an International Disarmament Organization within the framework of the United Nations to ensure compliance at all times with all disarmament obligations;

(d) The institution of effective means for the enforcement of international agreements, for the settlement of disputes, and for the maintenance of peace in accordance with the principles of the United Nations.

Call on the negotiating states:

(a) To develop the outline program set forth below into an agreed plan for general and complete disarmament and to continue their efforts without interruption until the whole program has been achieved;

(b) To this end to seek to attain the widest possible area of agreement at the earliest possible date;

(c) Also to seek — without prejudice to progress on the disarmament program — agreement on those immediate measures that would contribute to the common security of nations and that could facilitate and form a part of that program.

Affirm that disarmament negotiations should be guided by the following principles:

(a) Disarmament shall take place as rapidly as possible until it is completed in stages containing balanced, phased and safeguarded measures, with each measure and stage to be carried out in an agreed period of time.

(b) Compliance with all disarmament obligations shall be effectively verified from their entry into force. Verification arrangements shall be instituted progressively and in such a manner as to verify not only that agreed limitations or reductions take place but also that retained armed forces and armaments do not exceed agreed levels at any stage.

(c) Disarmament shall take place in a manner that will not affect adversely the security of any state, whether or not a party to an international agreement or treaty.

(d) As states relinquish their arms, the United Nations shall be progressively strengthened in order to improve its capacity to assure international security and the peaceful settlement of differences as well as to facilitate the development of international cooperation in common tasks for the benefit of mankind.

(e) Transition from one stage of disarmament to the next shall take place as soon as all the measures in the preceding stage have been carried out and effective verification is continuing and as soon as the arrangements that have been agreed to be necessary for the next stage have been instituted.

Agree upon the following outline program for achieving general and complete disarmament:

STAGE I

A. *To Establish an International Disarmament Organization:*

(a) An International Disarmament Organization (IDO) shall be established within the framework of the United Nations upon entry into force of the agreement. Its functions shall be expanded progressively as required for the effective verification of the disarmament program.

(b) The IDO shall have: (I) a General Conference of all the parties; (2) a Commission consisting of representatives of all the major powers as permanent members and certain other states on a rotating basis; and (3) an Administrator who will administer the Organization subject to the direction of the Commission and who will have the authority, staff, and finances adequate to assure effective impartial implementation of the functions of the Organization.

(c) The IDO shall: (I)ensure compliance with the obligations undertaken by verifying the execution of measures agreed upon; (2) assist the states in developing the details of agreed further verification and disarmament measures; (3) provide for the establishment of such bodies as may be necessary for working out the details of further measures provided for in the program and for such other expert study groups as may be required to give continuous study to the problems of disarmament; (4) receive reports on the progress of disarmament and verification arrangements and determine the transition from one stage to the next.

B. *To Reduce Armed Forces and Armaments:*

(a) Force levels shall be limited to 2.1 million each for the U.S. and U.S.S.R. and to appropriate levels not exceeding 2.1 million each for all other militarily significant states. Reductions to the agreed levels will proceed by equitable, proportionate, and verified steps.

(b) Levels of armaments of prescribed types shall be reduced by equitable and balanced steps. The reductions shall be accomplished by transfers of armaments to depots supervised by the IDO. When, at specified periods during the Stage I reduction process, the states party to the agreement have agreed that the armaments and armed forces are at prescribed levels, the armaments in depots shall be destroyed or converted to peaceful uses.

(c) The production of agreed types of armaments shall be limited.

(d) A Chemical, Biological, Radiological (CBR) Experts Commission shall be established within the IDO for the purpose of examining and reporting on the feasibility and means for accomplishing the verifiable reduction and eventual elimination of CBR weapons stockpiles and the halting of their production.

C. *To Contain and Reduce the Nuclear Threat:*

(a) States that have not acceded to a treaty effectively prohibiting the testing of nuclear weapons shall do so.

(b) The production of fissionable materials for use in weapons shall be stopped.

(c) Upon the cessation of production of fissionable materials for use in weapons, agreed initial quantities of fissionable material from past production shall be transferred to non-weapons purposes.

(d) Any fissionable materials transferred between countries for peaceful uses of nuclear energy shall be subject to appropriate safeguards to be developed in agreement with the IAEA.

(e) States owning nuclear weapons shall not relinquish control of such weapons to any nation not owning them and shall not transmit to any such nation information or material necessary for their manufacture. States not owning nuclear weapons shall not manufacture such weapons, attempt to obtain control of such weapons belonging to other states, or seek or receive information or materials necessary for their manufacture.

(f) A Nuclear Experts Commission consisting of representatives of the nuclear states shall be established within the IDO for the purpose of examining and reporting on the feasibility and means for accomplishing the verified reduction and eventual elimination of nuclear weapons stockpiles.

D. *To Reduce Strategic Nuclear Weapons Delivery Vehicles:*

(a) Strategic nuclear weapons delivery vehicles in specified categories and agreed types of weapons designed to counter such vehicles shall be reduced to agreed levels by equitable and balanced steps. The reduction shall be accomplished in each step by transfers to depots supervised by the IDO of vehicles that are in excess of levels agreed upon for each step. At specified periods during the Stage I reduction process, the vehicles that have been placed under supervision of the IDO shall be destroyed or converted to peaceful uses.

(b) Production of agreed categories of strategic nuclear weapons delivery vehicles and agreed types of weapons designed to counter such vehicles shall be discontinued or limited.

(c) Testing of agreed categories of strategic nuclear weapons delivery vehicles and agreed types of weapons designed to counter such vehicles shall be limited or halted.

E. *To Promote the Peaceful Use of Outer Space:*

(a) The placing into orbit or stationing in outer space of weapons capable of producing mass destruction shall be prohibited.

(b) States shall give advance notification to participating states and to the IDO of launchings of space vehicles and missiles, together with the track of the vehicle.

F. *To Reduce the Risks of War by Accident, Miscalculation, and Surprise Attack:*

(a) States shall give advance notification to the participating states and to the IDO of major military movements and maneuvers, on a scale as may be agreed, which might give rise to misinterpretation or cause alarm and induce countermeasures. The notification shall include the geographic areas to be used and the nature, scale and time span of the event.

(b) There shall be established observation posts at such locations as major ports, railway centers, motor highways, and air bases to report on concentrations and movements of military forces.

(c) There shall also be established such additional inspection arrangements to reduce the danger of surprise attack as may be agreed.

(d) An international commission shall be established immediately within the IDO to examine and make recommendations on the possibility of further measures to reduce the risks of nuclear war by accident, miscalculation, or failure of communication.

G. *To Keep the Peace:*

(a) States shall reaffirm their obligations under the U.N. Charter to refrain from the threat or use of any type of armed force — including nuclear, conventional, or CBR — contrary to the principles of the U.N. Charter.

(b) States shall agree to refrain from indirect aggression and subversion against any country.

(c) States shall use all appropriate processes for the peaceful settlement of disputes and shall seek within the United Nations further arrangements for the peaceful settlement of international disputes and for the codification and progressive development of international law.

(d) States shall develop arrangements in Stage I for the establishment in Stage II of a U.N. Peace Force.

(e) A U.N. peace observation group shall be staffed with a standing cadre of observers who could be despatched to investigate any situation which might constitute a threat to or breach of the peace.

STAGE II

A. ***International Disarmament Organization:***

The powers and responsibilities of the IDO shall be progressively enlarged in order to give it the capabilities to verify the measures undertaken in Stage II.

B. ***To Further Reduce Armed Forces and Armaments:***

(a) Levels of forces for the U.S., U.S.S.R., and other militarily significant states shall be further reduced by substantial amounts to agreed levels in equitable and balanced steps.

(b) Levels of armaments of prescribed types shall be further reduced by equitable and balanced steps. The reduction shall be accomplished by transfers of armaments to depots supervised by the IDO. When, at specified periods during the Stage II reduction process, the parties have agreed that the armaments and armed forces are at prescribed levels, the armaments in depots shall be destroyed or converted to peaceful uses.

(c) There shall be further agreed restrictions on the production of armaments.

(d) Agreed military bases and facilities wherever they are located shall be dismantled or converted to peaceful uses.

(e) Depending upon the findings of the Experts Commission on CBR weapons, the production of CBR weapons shall be halted, existing stocks progressively reduced, and the resulting excess quantities destroyed or converted to peaceful uses.

C. ***To Further Reduce the Nuclear Threat:***

Stocks of nuclear weapons shall be progressively reduced to the minimum levels which can be agreed upon as a result of the findings of the Nuclear Experts Commission; the resulting excess of fissionable material shall be transferred to peaceful purposes.

D. ***To Further Reduce Strategic Nuclear Weapons Delivery Vehicles:***

Further reductions in the stocks of strategic nuclear weapons delivery vehicles and agreed types of weapons designed to counter such vehicles shall be carried out in accordance with the procedure outlined in Stage I.

E. ***To Keep the Peace:***

During Stage II, states shall develop further the peace-keeping processes of the United Nations, to the end that the United Nations can effectively in Stage III deter or suppress any threat or use of force in violation of the purposes and principles of the United Nations:

(a) States shall agree upon strengthening the structure, authority, and operation of the United Nations so as to assure that the United Nations will be able effectively to protect states against threats to or breaches of the peace.

(b) The U.N. Peace Force shall be established and progressively strengthened.

(c) States shall also agree upon further improvements and developments in rules of international conduct and in processes for peaceful settlement of disputes and differences.

STAGE III

By the time Stage II has been completed, the confidence produced through a verified disarmament program, the acceptance of rules of peaceful international behavior, and the development of strengthened international peace-keeping processes within the framework of the U.N. should have reached a point where the states of the world can move forward to Stage III. In Stage III progressive controlled disarmament and continuously developing principles and procedures of international law would proceed to a point where no state would have the military power to challenge the progressively strengthened U.N. Peace Force and all international disputes would be settled according to the agreed principles of international conduct.

The progressive steps to be taken during the final phase of the disarmament program would be directed toward the attainment of a world in which:

(a) States would retain only those forces, non-nuclear armaments, and establishments required for the purpose of maintaining internal order; they would also support and provide agreed manpower for a U.N. Peace Force.

(b) The U.N. Peace Force, equipped with agreed types and quantities of armaments, would be fully functioning.

(c) The manufacture of armaments would be prohibited except for those of agreed types and quantities to be used by the U.N. Peace Force and those required to maintain internal order. All other armaments would be destroyed or converted to peaceful purposes.

(d) The peace-keeping capabilities of the United Nations would be sufficiently strong and the obligations of all states under such arrangements sufficiently far-reaching as to assure peace and the just settlement of differences in a disarmed world.

Notes

— Chapter 1 —
Changing the Role of America's Armed Forces

1. See "Insider Report," *The New American*, July 11, 1994, p. 10.
2. Bradley Graham, "New Twist for U.S. Troops: Peace Maneuvers," *Washington Post*, August 15, 1995.
3. Eric Schmitt, "Military Planning an Expanded Role For the Reserves," *New York Times*, November 25, 1994.
4. Randolph Ryan, "General unfazed by US Army training slowdown," *Boston Globe*, November 29, 1994.
5. Editorial, "Loathing the military in peace and war," *Washington Times*, July 3, 1994.
6. John Lancaster, "Accused of Ridiculing Clinton, General Faces Air Force Probe," *Washington Post*, June 8, 1994.
7. Richard Grenier, "The end of the rugged individualists?", *Washington Times*, June 15, 1994.
8. Associated Press, "Gore, in letters as a student, scorned Army," *Boston Globe*, November 21, 1994.
9. Robert D. Novak, "Blue Helmets for Americans," *Washington Post*, April 25, 1994.

— Chapter 2 —
World Government or American Independence?

1. Grenville Clark and Louis B. Sohn, *World Peace Through World Law*, Second Edition (Cambridge, MA: Harvard University Press, 1962).
2. Walt W. Rostow, *The United States in the World Arena* (New York: Harper Brothers, 1960).
3. Lincoln P. Bloomfield, *A World Effectively Controlled by the United Nations*, Institute For Defense Analysis, March 10, 1962, State Department Contract No. SCC 28270.
4. William Fulbright, *Old Myths and New Realities* (New York: Random House, 1964).

— Chapter 3 —
The UN's Noose Tightens

1. Senator Simon's speech to the Senate; *Congressional Record*, January 10, 1991, pp. S107-108.
2. Anthony Lewis, "Not in a Single Man," *New York Times*, September 12, 1994.
3. John Hart Ely, "Clinton, Congress and War," *New York Times*, October 23, 1993.
4. For a survey of George Bush's long association with the organization promoting the new world order's world government see James J. Drummey, *The Establishment's Man* (Appleton, WI: Western Islands, 1991). See also John F. McManus, *The Insiders* (Appleton, WI: The John Birch Society, 1995).
5. See William F. Jasper, *Global Tyranny ... Step By Step* (Appleton, WI: Western Islands, 1992); Robert W. Lee, *The United Nations Conspiracy* (Appleton, WI: Western Islands, 1981); and G. Edward Griffin, *The Fearful Master, A Second Look at the United Nations* (Appleton, WI: Western Islands, 1964).
6. Associated Press release, "Some U.S. troops face foreign control," *Bakersfield Californian*, May 30, 1991.
7. Barbara Crossette, "Congress Scrutinizes Peacekeeping Test Case," *New York Times*, March 1, 1992.
8. Samuel Francis, "We can't even decide for ourselves whether or not to go to war?" *Washington Times*, August 5, 1994.

9. Bradley Graham, "New Twist for U.S. Troops: Peace Maneuvers," *Washington Post*, August 15, 1994.
10. Kevin McElroy, "Base reaches global proportions," *South Jersey Courier-Post*, October 2, 1994.
11. Douglas Jehl, "25,000 U.S. Troops To Aid U.N. Force If It Quits Bosnia," *New York Times*, December 9, 1994.
12. John F. Harris and Bradley Graham, "U.S. to Send Marine Force to Protect U.N. Troops as They Leave Somalia," *Washington Post*, December 17, 1994.
13. "Supplement to *An Agenda For Peace*: Position Paper of the Secretary General on the Occasion of the Fiftieth Anniversary of the United Nations" (United Nations Document A/50/60; S/1995/1; January 3, 1995).
14. Ron Fournier, "Clinton won't deploy Guard in US capital," *Boston Globe*, October 26, 1993.
15. David Beard, "Military Fighting Crime in Puerto Rican Housing Projects," *Albuquerque Journal*, October 3, 1993.
16. Bob Greene, "Is it time to send UN troops to U.S.?", *Chicago Tribune*, September 29, 1993.
17. Catherine O'Neill, "Bring in the Army to End the Fear," *Los Angeles Times*, March 29, 1994.
18. Charles J. Hanley, "For 1st Time, U.N. Turns Focus to Gun Control," *Manchester* (NH) *Union Leader*, May 24, 1994.

— Chapter 4 —
The Constitution Authorizes an Army and a Navy

1. Cited in Stephen E. Ambrose, *Duty, Honor, Country: A History of West Point* (Baltimore, MD: The Johns Hopkins Press, 1966).

— Chapter 5 —
Congress, the President, the Military, and the Constitution

1. Jonathan Elliot (ed.), *The Debates in the Several State Conventions on the Adoption of the Federal Constitution*, 5 Volumes (Philadelphia, PA: J. B. Lippincott, 1901).
2. Paul Leicester Ford, *The Writings of Thomas Jefferson*, 10 volumes (New York: G.P. Putnam's Sons, 1899).
3. Gaillard Hunt and James Brown Scott, *The Debates in the Federal Constitution of 1787 by James Madison* (New York: Oxford University Press, 1920).
4. Ellen C. Collier, *Instances of Use of United States Armed Forces Abroad, 1793-1993* (Document #93-890 F, October 7, 1993, Congressional Research Service, Library of Congress, Washington DC).
5. Roy P. Basler, Editor, *The Collected Works of Abraham Lincoln, Volume 1* (New Brunswick, NJ: Rutgers University Press, 1953).

— Chapter 6 —
Inviting Homosexuals Invites Destruction

1. "Gay Activists Summon Their Hopes, Resolves," *Washington Post*, April 18, 1993.
2. *U.S. Constitution*, Article I, Section 8, Clause 14.
3. Michael Hedges, "Marine ready to end career to protest policy change," *Washington Times*, June 24, 1994
4. Chris Reidy, "Just saying no," *Boston Globe*, January 31, 1993.
5. Quoted by William Matthews, *Air Force Times*, July 20, 1992.
6. Cited by Ronald D. Ray, *Military Necessity & Homosexuality, Afterword* (Louisville, KY: First Principles Press, 1993).
7. *Time*, July 26, 1993.
8. Ronald D. Ray, *Military Necessity and Homosexuality* (Louisville, KY: First Principles Press, 1993).
9. Ronald D. Ray, "Virtue: The First Principle of American Naval Service Since 1775, Surrendered in 1993," unpublished essay, 1993.
10. *Baltimore Sun*, January 11, 1993.
11. Ronald D. Ray, *Military Necessity and Homosexuality — Afterword*, op. cit.
12. *Facts on File*, August 11, 1993.
13. Ray, op. cit.
14. Ibid.

— Chapter 7 —
War Is No Place For Women

1. Brian Mitchell, *Weak Link: The Feminization of the American Military* (Washington, DC: Regnery Gateway, 1989).
2. James H. Webb, Jr., "Women Can't Fight," *Washingtonian* magazine, November 1969.

— Chapter 8 —
Creating War to Build Power and Destroy Freedom

1. See: Hearings, U.S. Congress, House of Representatives, Special Committee to Investigate Tax-Exempt Foundations and Comparable Organizations, 83rd Congress, Second Session, 1954; William H. McIlhany II, *The Tax-Exempt Foundations* (Westport, CT: Arlington House, 1980); *The Hidden Agenda,* a video presentation containing Norman Dodd's in-person account (Westlake Village, CA: American Media, 1991); and Rene A. Wormser, *Foundations* (New York: Devin-Adair Co., 1958).
2. George Sylvester Viereck, *The Strangest Friendship in History* (New York: Liveright, 1926).
3. Charles Seymour, *The Intimate Papers of Colonel House* (Boston, MA: Houghton Miflin, 1926).
4. Colin Simpson, *The Lusitania* (Boston, MA: Little, Brown & Co., 1972).
5. James Perloff, *The Shadows of Power* (Appleton, WI: Western Islands, 1988).
6. "Report of the Special Committee on Tax-Exempt Foundations," Government Printing Office, December 15, 1954, as cited in Dan Smoot, *The Invisible Government* (Appleton, WI: Western Islands, 1965).
7. *Postwar Foreign Policy Preparation, 1939-1945*, U.S. State Department; *Interlocking Subversion in Government Departments*, U.S. Senate Internal Security Subcommittee report, July 30, 1953.
8. G. Edward Griffin, *The Fearful Master: A Second Look At the United Nations* (Appleton, WI: Western Islands, 1964).
9. *Congressional Record — Senate*, July 27, 1945, p. 8122.
10. *Congressional Record-Senate*, July 27, 1945, pp. 8188-8189.
11. Bob Dole, "Peacekeepers and Politics," *New York Times*, January 24, 1994.

— Chapter 9 —
NATO and Korea; SEATO and Vietnam

1. Available evidence shows that world government advocates in and out of our own government participated in every step of communism's rise to power. The Wilson/House administration supplied critical diplomatic assistance to Trotsky during his 1917 return to Russia. U.S. "humanitarian" aid saved the Bolsheviks in the 1920s; financial and diplomatic aid rescued them in the 1930s; wartime "Lend Lease" built them into a world power in the 1940s; and transfers of equipment, technology and money did everything possible to keep them afloat and build their power all during the era of the "Cold War." See John F. McManus, *An Overview Of Our World* (Appleton, WI: The John Birch Society, 1971); Gary Allen, *None Dare Call It Conspiracy* (Rossmoor, CA: Concord Press, 1972); Antony Sutton, *Wall Street and the Bolshevik Revolution* (New Rochelle, NY: Arlington House, 1974); and Antony Sutton, *National Suicide: Military Aid To the Soviet Union* (New Rochelle, NY: Arlington House, 1973).
2. *Congressional Record — Senate*, June 28, 1950, p. 9322.
3. Ibid.
4. Ibid., p. 9323.
5. Noted in Department of State *Bulletin*, Volume 23, Number 575, July 10, 1950.
6. *Congressional Record — Senate*, June 28, 1950, p. 9320.
7. Cited in Justin Raimondo, *Reclaiming the American Right* (Burlingame, CA: Center For Libertarian Studies, 1993).
8. Matthew B. Ridgway, *The Korean War* (New York: Doubleday & Company, 1967).
9. Douglas MacArthur, *Reminiscences* (New York: Time, Inc., 1964).

10. "Interlocking Subversion in Government Departments," Hearings, U.S. Senate Internal Security Subcommittee, 1954; "Military Situation in the Far East," Committee on Armed Forces, 1951.
11. Mark Clark, *From the Danube To the Yalu* (New York: Harper & Brothers, 1954).
12. Hearings, op cit.
13. James Stockdale, *In Love & War* (New York: Harper & Row, 1984).
14. Keith William Nolan, *Operation Buffalo* (New York: Dell Publishing, 1992).
15. *Congressional Record*, March 6, 14, and 18, 1985.
16. Wallis W. Wood, "Vietnam: While Brave Men Die," *American Opinion*, June 1967.
17. Wallis W. Wood, "It's Treason!", *American Opinion*, May 1968.

— Chapter 10 —
Disarmament for All Except the UN

1. Rep. Ted Weiss (D-NY) joyfully cited this letter in his statement to the House appearing in the *Congressional Record*, May 25, 1982, pp. H2840-49. The entire text of the "Blueprint" is reproduced in these pages.
2. Letter from Luis Fernando Jaramillo, the Permanent Representative of Colombia to the United Nations, addressed to the Secretary of the Disarmament Commission, March 21, 1994.
3. Clark and Sohn, op cit.
4. John Kennedy insisted that he belonged to the CFR although his name never appeared on any CFR roster. On June 7, 1960, Mr. Kennedy, then a U.S. Senator, responded by letter to an inquiry about his membership in the Council. He wrote: "I am a member of the Council on Foreign Relations in New York City. As a long-time subscriber to the quarterly *Foreign Affairs*, and as a member of the Senate, I was invited to become a member." See Dan Smoot, *The Invisible Government* (Appleton, WI: Western Islands, 1977 ed.).
5. Richard N. Gardner, *In Pursuit of World Order* (New York: Frederick A. Praeger, 1964).
6. Trygve Lie, *In the Cause of Peace* (New York: Macmillan Company, 1954).
7. *Interlocking Subversion in Government Department*, Hearings, op cit.

— Chapter 11 —
Politicizing the Generals and Admirals

1. Complete text of this speech appears in the *Congressional Record*, Dec. 15, 1987, pp. S18145-50.
2. See George Sylvester Viereck. *The Strangest Friendship in History* (New York: Liveright, 1932).
3. Phyllis Schlafly and Chester Ward, *Kissinger on the Couch* (New Rochelle, NY: Arlington House, 1975).
4. See Perloff, *The Shadows of Power*, op cit.
5. J. Anthony Lukas, "The Council on Foreign Relations: Is it a Club? Seminar? Presidium? Invisible Government?", *New York Times Magazine*, November 21, 1971.
6. Excerpt from March 12, 1990 speech by Paul Nitze, *Wall Street Journal*, April 10, 1990.
7. Susan L.M. Huck, "Lost Valor: The C.F.R. in Our Armed Forces," *American Opinion*, October 1977.

— Chapter 12 —
POW Abandonment Affects Morale

1. Report of U.S. Senate Committee on Foreign Relations Republican Staff, "An Examination of U.S. Policy Toward POW/MIAs," May 23, 1991 (hereinafter noted as Republican Staff Report).
2. Associated Press dispatch, Washington, DC, March 8, 1973, as reported in Republican Staff Report, op cit.
3. *Washington Post*, February 18, 1973.
4. Associated Press dispatch, March 8, 1973, op cit.
5. William F. Jasper, "Bring Them Home!", *The New American*, September 24, 1991.

6. Republican Staff Report, op cit.
7. Ibid.
8. Miles Z. Epstein and T. Douglas Donaldson, "POW-MIAs, The Men We Left Behind," *The American Legion* magazine, March 1992.
9. Stuart A. Harrington, *Peace With Honor? An American Reports on Vietnam, 1973-1975* (San Rafael, CA: Presidio Press, 1983).
10. Epstein and Douglas, op cit.
11. Republican Staff Report, op cit.
12. Ibid.

— Chapter 13 —
Get US Out! of the United Nations

1. Linda Hossie, "U.N. lacks plan for trial after warlord's capture," *Washington Times*, June 20, 1993.
2. Dr. T. Vleurinck, Editor, *46 Angry Men: The 46 Civilian Doctors of Elizabethville Denounce U.N.O. Violations in Katanga* (Brussels, Belgium: 96 Avenue de Broqueville, 1962; Belmont, MA: American Opinion, 1962).
3. A more complete recounting of the UN's deadly action against Katanga appears in G. Edward Griffin's *The Fearful Master: A Second Look at the United Nations* (Appleton, WI: Western Islands, 1964). See also Smith Hempstone, *Rebels, Mercenaries and Dividends* (New York: Frederic A. Praeger, Inc., 1962). Hempstone, a correspondent for the *Chicago News*, provides an eyewitness account of the UN's atrocities.
4. Senator Thomas Dodd (D-CT), *Congressional Record*, September 16, 1961.
5. Ibid.
6. Charles Krauthammer, "The Immaculate Intervention," *Time*, July 26, 1993.
7. *Washington Post*, November 12, 1994.
8. *Washington Times*, February 26, 1994.
9. Paul Lewis, "Sex Scandal Roils UNICEF Unit," *New York Times*, June 25, 1987; "Staff of U.N. Children's Fund Sentenced in Child Sex Case," Reuters dispatch from Brussels, March 7, 1988.
10. Doug Nassif, "Congressman Charges UNICEF with Funding Indochina Communist Effort," *National Catholic Register*, September 14, 1975.
11. Associated Press release, *Los Angeles Times*, September 25, 1964.
12. Lt. Cdr. Michael J. Walsh, USN (Ret.), *SEAL!* (New York: Pocket Books, 1994).
13. *Washington Times*, January 28, 1994.
14. Krauthammer, op cit.
15. Keith B. Richburg, "Italy, in Rebuke to U.N., to Yank Troops From Mogadishu," *Washington Post*, August 14, 1993.
16. Michael R. Gordon, "U.S. Officers Were Split on Botched Somali Raid," *New York Times*, May 13, 1994.)
17. Article by Julia Preston, *Washington Post*, October 9, 1993. For a complete survey of the ambitious and frightening plans of UN Secretary General Boutros-Ghali, we highly recommend William F. Jasper's *Global Tyranny ... Step By Step* (Appleton, WI: Western Islands, 1992).
18. See William F. Jasper, "Behind Our Defeat in Somalia," *The New American*, September 5, 1994.

Index

Acknowledgements

No book can ever be written without the input, encouragement and professional help of numerous individuals. To name some would undoubtedly place me in the unwanted position of having to apologize for forgetting one or more. Being somewhat forgetful, I beg to be allowed a more general expression of gratitude.

My thanks go to the researchers, typesetters, editors, and project managers who shepherded me and the book through to completion. I thank my colleagues in The John Birch Society who had confidence enough to entrust the responsibility of this undertaking to me. And I thank our Society's members for enabling me to spend so much of my life's efforts in the great endeavor that has brought us together.

As I wrote, I thought of many teachers who helped me to understand and use the English language. I owe a great deal to them.

I have had occasion over recent months to recall much about my three years of Marine Corps duty, the many wonderful men with whom I served, and the proud history of that unique branch of the U.S. armed forces. I am indebted to many for having had the privilege of wearing "the globe and anchor."

I owe mountains of gratitude to a superb family whose patience and love have always been a source of strength and whose support of me and personal sacrifices for me have always been an inspiration.

And I owe a tremendous debt to those noble and far-seeing individuals who crafted the greatest nation in all history — the United States of America — whose preservation in liberty is the underlying reason for the creation of this book.

About the Author

John F. McManus graduated in 1957 with a Bachelor of Science degree in Physics from Holy Cross College in Worcester, Massachusetts. At graduation he received a commission as a Lieutenant, United States Marine Corps, and served on active duty for three years. For six years, he was employed as an electronics engineer in New England.

Mr. McManus joined the staff of the John Birch Society in 1966. In 1973, he became the organization's director of public relations and its chief media representative throughout the United States. He has appeared on hundreds of radio and television programs, including C-SPAN and the Larry King Show.

Also in 1973, Mr. McManus began writing and syndicating a weekly newspaper column entitled *The Birch Log*. He has authored and produced numerous audiovisual programs and written extensively for JBS-affiliated publications. His book *The Insiders* has gone through four editions. His most recent book prior to *Changing Commands* was *Financial Terrorism — Hijacking America Under the Threat of Bankruptcy* in which he explained the economic problems facing our nation and how they can be solved. He is in wide demand as a speaker.

Mr. McManus is the publisher of *The New American* magazine, a biweekly journal of news and commentary. In June 1991, he was named President of the John Birch Society.

Recommended Reading

Global Tyranny ... Step By Step .... **pb $12.95**
WILLIAM F. JASPER — A counterpart to *Financial Terrorism*. Thoroughly documents the plan to build the United Nations into a world tyranny. Extremely compelling. (1992 ed., 350 pp.)

The Shadows Of Power .... **pb $10.95**
JAMES PERLOFF — An exposé of the Council on Foreign Relations and its tragic impact on American foreign policy. Compiled from the group's own documents. Highly recommended. (1988 ed., 266 pp.)

The Insiders .... **pb $3.00**
JOHN F. MCMANUS — A look at the powerful few who really dictate America's policies. Spotlights the Council on Foreign Relations and Trilateral Commission. (1995 ed., 152 pp.)

Financial Terrorism .... **pb $8.95**
JOHN F. MCMANUS — The Insiders' plan to hijack America through debt, inflation, entitlements, and the Fed. (1993 ed., 288 pp.)

The Law .... **pb $3.95**
FREDERIC BASTIAT — Arguably the best essay ever written on the proper role of government. Bastiat, a French statesman and economist, confronted socialist tyranny in the middle 1800s. (75 pp.)

The Blue Book Of The John Birch Society .... **pb $5.95**
ROBERT WELCH — The transcript of the entire two-day presentation that launched this organization in 1958. (1992 ed., 202 pp.)

John Birch Society Introductory Packet **$5.00**
Numerous pamphlets analyzing current events, a sample *JBS Bulletin*, and a sample of *The New American* magazine.

The New American .... **(see below)**
The New American magazine, a biweekly publication affiliated with The John Birch Society, is must reading for those who would be truly informed about the plans and programs of the Insiders.

- **Six-months subscription** **$22.00**
- **One-year subscription** **$39.00**

(Please contact *The New American* for foreign rates.)

Except for subscriptions to *The New American*, please add 15 percent for postage and handling ($2.00 minimum).

American Opinion Book Services
P.O. Box 8040 • Appleton, WI 54913
(Credit card orders accepted at 414–749–3783.)